Jane Ferguson

MODERN DISASTERS

D1823812

Hippo Books
Scholastic Publications Limited
London

Scholastic Publications Ltd.,
10 Earlham Street, London WC2H 9RX, UK

Scholastic Inc.,
730 Broadway, New York, NY 10003, USA

Scholastic Tab Publications Ltd.,
123 Newkirk Road, Richmond Hill
Ontario L4C 3G5, Canada

Ashton Scholastic Pty. Ltd.,
PO Box 579, Gosford, New South Wales,
Australia

Ashton Scholastic Ltd.,
165 Marua Road, Panmure, Auckland 6,
New Zealand

First published under the title *A Book of Disasters*, 1981
This amended edition published by
Scholastic Publications Limited, 1988

Copyright © Jane Ferguson, 1981 and 1988

ISBN 0 590 70935 6

All rights reserved

Made and printed by Giethoon, Holland
Typeset in Linotron Times by
J&L Composition Ltd, Filey, North Yorkshire

This book is sold subject to the condition that it shall not, by way of
trade or otherwise be lent, resold, hired out, or otherwise circulated
without the publisher's prior consent in any form of binding or cover
other than that in which it is published and without a similar condition,
including this condition, being imposed upon the subsequent
purchaser.

MODERN DISASTERS

Chernobyl, Ethiopia, Heysel, Kings Cross – these names still haunt us with memories of terrible catastrophes that occurred there, with the senseless loss of human life. Jane Ferguson brings these and other great disasters of the twentieth century closer to us. How did the accidents occur in the first place? Could they have been prevented? What are the human stories behind the disasters? And most importantly, can anything be done to lessen the chances of similarly horrifying tragedies happening in the future?

Contents

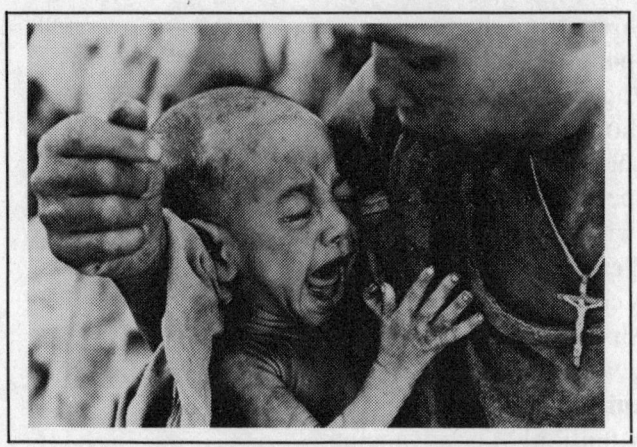

Introduction

You know far more about the world than your grandparents ever did. Not only has television taken us to every country under the sun, but nearly all of us know people whose old homes are far, far away in places that were once-just boring names in geography. An earthquake in Mexico, a famine in Mozambique, a flood in Bangladesh – no longer can such horrors be simply short paragraphs in a newspaper. Today the victims have familiar faces, and we all share their grief. Ordinary people rush to help far-distant countries in a way they never did before.

This is a book about modern disasters. There are more of us living on earth than ever, so each accident, whether in nature or involving machines, kills or hurts more people. Villages become towns, and towns densely packed cities. Planes carry more passengers, and tankers more oil. Science is now highly sophisticated, and has produced chemicals that will remain deadly into infinity.

The impact of natural disasters, especially in the poor countries of the Third World, has increased more than six-fold in your lifetime. But this isn't because there are six times more droughts, say, or even six times as many people, but, because of the conditions they live in, those people become victims more easily. The setting for a disaster already existed in Ethiopia and the drought simply tipped the country over the edge, and in Central or South America, earthquakes take the greatest toll among the slums.

No one can stop an earthquake or a volcano, but the effects of such natural disasters can be – and nearly always are – made much worse by the decisions of *people*.

Perhaps we feel that disasters are too awful to think about, and after a while we start believing they could never happen. Just as for centuries farmers have returned again and again to fertile soil around an active volcano, so today the people of southern California and Japan build their homes, schools, hospitals and power supplies over earthquake faults they *know* will shake again. In 1987 the 6.1 quake in Los Angeles, where two-thirds of the state's population lives, was just a reminder.

Back in the seventies scientists already suspected that the ozone layer in the earth's atmosphere, which stops ultraviolet radiation from reaching us, was being destroyed by the chlorine released in the chlorofluorocarbons (CFCs) used to make aerosol sprays, foam packaging (like hamburger cartons) and the workings of fridges. The resulting radiation is a threat to all life-forms, bringing more skin cancers and catastrophic changes to our climate patterns.

The United States banned CFCs in 1978, but Europe wouldn't listen. Ten years later the British government was still stalling, even though the hole in the ozone layer over Antarctica is now the size of the USA and the depth of Mount Everest. When we can't actually see anything happening, or when the danger seems to belong to the future, industry and governments find it simpler to pretend it's not really there.

These are grand-scale examples, but everyday decisions of ordinary men and women can also cause a disaster: ignoring fire regulations, taking a risk to catch up on a timetable, not wanting to be the one to raise a false alarm, or – over and over again – not wanting to spend more money. Because it just doesn't seem possible that anything could really happen.

Our modern lifestyle increases the risks. Everyone naturally wants to be warm and fed and comfortable, and we all, in rich countries and in poor, take risks to make it so. We are still stripping the earth, altering the balance of animal life and even our weather, polluting the land and sea, and searching for cheaper fuel without counting the cost in lives. We believe experts who talk of foolproof safety, though we see for ourselves endless examples of unpredictable behaviour in both humans and materials.

All accidents are unexpected! They all turn out to have some weird, usually small and silly, starting-point. Psychologists agree that the over-confidence of the Russian engineers contributed to the Chernobyl fire, and that this applies to "experts" everywhere. In 1980 in America the very first steps of a nuclear war were set in motion by a simple fault in a cheap microcircuit: we know now that since 1971 there have been 151 occasions in the nuclear business when, for a little while, something went seriously wrong.

You, the young, are the guardians of the future. Don't be frightened. Don't be scared to ask questions, or feel you have to believe what those "in charge" tell you. Don't think your opinions don't count, or that you're too unimportant to do anything. Remember that, just as it is always people who, by carelessness, greed or lack of planning, turn accidents into disasters, so is it also people – people like you – who can lessen the horrors, or even prevent them altogether.

Take-off for terror

"There were loads of kids on board. Everyone was screaming, shouting and pushing. Some people fell on the floor and were trampled on. They were diving out of their seats and everyone was pushing."

It was August 1985, and twenty-one-year-old Keith Middleton was going on holiday with his girlfriend. As their British Airtours Boeing 737-200 was taking off from Manchester Airport the port engine exploded, rupturing the fuel tank in the wing. Within minutes thick, black, deadly smoke had filled the plane. In the panic and terror fifty-five people died, including some of the cabin crew who selflessly saved other people.

The engine fault was traced to the combusters, which ignite the air and fuel in the combustion chamber. It was an American Pratt and Whitney engine of a type that was already involved in a series of safety checks after earlier fires. Interestingly, two years later, a McDonnell Douglas MD-80 with the same JT8D engine crashed in flames during take-off at Detroit in America, though later inquiries found no connection.

The Detroit plane skidded along an airport road, so there were motorists among the 154 who died. A little four-year-old girl was the sole survivor: she lost both parents and her six-year-old brother, and it was only the TV publicity about her chipped tooth and lavender-painted nails that made her grandmother realize who she must be.

Today some critics believe airlines care less about safety than profits. Many planes, especially holiday charters, still have more seats than they were designed to carry – the Manchester plane had 130 instead of 115 – and there is still a row of extra seats next to the overwing exits of 737s.

We used to think that aircraft heated to "flashover" (or total combustion) in two minutes, but now we know passengers do survive the heat and can try to escape. Smoke from burning seats is

highly poisonous, but smoke hoods over their heads would protect them for about twenty minutes, and reduce the dangerous panic.

The cost of hoods would add a tiny amount to a £100 fare, but forty people in the Manchester horror might still be alive if they had remained conscious and all the exits had been clear.

Three years later, the British Civil Aviation Authority still insisted these suggestions would make too little difference to be worth forcing them on airlines.

13

Love letters in the sky

One day in 1978 a Japan Air Lines 747 had a minor accident, scraping its tail along the ground as it landed. Government inspectors, without checking, approved incorrect repairs by Boeing technicians. Slowly, invisibly, other cracks developed.

Seven years later, on August 12, 1985, that JAL 747 killed 520 people in the worst-ever single plane crash. Soon after it left Tokyo, pressurized air escaped through cracks in the rear bulkhead into the tail, which disintegrated and destroyed all the

rudder controls.

For thirty-two minutes the plane dived and circled out of control, then crashed on a remote mountain ninety-seven kilometres away. Almost certainly some of the passengers survived, but because of bungling and squabbling among the air force and local police about who should rescue them, it took over fifteen hours to reach the site, and by then only four were still alive.

Eight-year-old Mikiko saved her mother by urging her to stay awake after her father, brother and sister had died; while twelve-year-old Keiko's father comforted her as she heard her little sister cry, "It hurts, it hurts," before he and her sister died. Although the fourth survivor, an off-duty stewardess, spoke of the "screaming panic" on board, some people managed to scribble farewells to their loved ones.

"To my three kids: take care of your mother. The aircraft is nose-diving. There is no hope. It was a happy life for me. Thank you all. God help us – goodbye."

Twelve-year-old Keiko is rescued from the crash

The warning no one listened to

Disasters such as air crashes seem to get relentlessly bigger as the years pass: each "worst ever" is soon surpassed in horror.

In March 1974 the worst air disaster ever – till then – happened over a forest on the outskirts of Paris. And it should *not* have happened, if

the lesson from an alarmingly close accident two years earlier had been learnt. At that time a DC-10 jumbo jet had avoided disaster only by good luck after a loader had trouble closing a cargo door.

This time a cargo door on a Turkish Airline DC-10 jet had been insecurely latched – it was later stated to be a design fault on these McDonnell Douglas planes – and it blew off in mid-air. The resulting sudden decompression sucked out six passengers still strapped to their seats, and seventy-two seconds later the plane crashed, killing everyone on board, most of whom were British.

Nobody in authority had the imagination or common sense to recognize the warning of that first near-disaster, which might have saved 346 lives.

Collision over a city

Air traffic controllers world-wide are worried about our overcrowded skies.

America has a dangerous shortage of controllers after strikers were sacked by President Reagan and airline deregulation led to certain airports being heavily overloaded. British controllers handle three million aircraft a year with what they say is old and unreliable equipment: they fear ever-increasing flights mean a growing number of near-misses ("near-hits" would be more accurate). With most airports close to cities, it is amazing that so few planes crash on to our streets and houses. But it can happen. . .

In a snowstorm over New York, one day in December 1960, a United Airlines DC-8 jet, flying in from Chicago, collided with a TWA Constellation from Ohio.

The DC-8 burst into flames as it fell on Brooklyn, killing eight people on the ground, destroying flats and setting shops and a chapel on fire – but miraculously missing a school of 1,700 children.

The Constellation fell into the harbour by Staten Island, across the bay from Brooklyn, wrecking some houses. It had been the worst mid-air crash known, and all but one of the 127 people on board the two planes died immediately.

However the sole survivor lived for only one more day. He was eleven years old, and before he died he described what it was like:

"I remember looking out of the plane window at the snow below covering the city. It looked like a picture out of a fairy book. It was a beautiful sight. Then, suddenly there was an explosion. The plane started to fall and people started to scream. I held on to my seat and then the plane crashed. That's all I remember."

The teams who lost against death

Some of the greatest names in Peruvian football have played for Alianza Lima. In December 1987 the club were coming home from a 1–0 win that kept them top of the First Division, when their plane plunged into the Pacific ten kilometres from Lima airport.

Twenty-eight players, plus nine from the management team, died in the crash, robbing Peru of six internationals and drastically affecting their chances of qualifying for the 1990 World Cup.

It was an echo of the tragic crash at ice-bound Munich airport in February 1958 which killed most of the Manchester United team, one of the best ever assembled. Bobby Charlton and manager Matt Busby were among the few to survive: the whole football world mourned "Busby's Babes", most of them little more than twenty.

In 1961 an air disaster

wiped out the American figure-skating team, and in March 1980 a jet crashed near Warsaw airport, Poland, killing everyone, including the entire amateur boxing team of the United States, their doctors, coaches and referees.

Perhaps sports teams, like a royal family or top-level government group, should consider travelling separately?

The worst air crash of all

The greatest air disaster of all – almost as awful as it's possible to get – happened on the ground.

In winter in the northern part of the world many people search out the sun in the holiday resorts of the Canary Islands, off the west coast of Africa. But they too can suffer from bad weather and fog. On March 27, 1977,

the airport on Tenerife had extra problems with planes diverted from neighbouring Las Palmas, which had been closed because of a terrorist bomb. And Tenerife had no ground radar to deal with such a situation.

Somehow, in the delay and confusion, two mighty jumbo jets prepared to take off from the same runway...

A Dutch KLM plane, carrying 249 people, roared down the runway at over 250 kph and ran straight into a waiting American Pan-Am Boeing 747, carrying 378 passengers and sixteen crew. Everyone on the Dutch plane died. About eighty people, lucky enough to be in the front or very back of the Boeing, got out, but many of these died later. Altogether, almost 570 people were killed in this catastrophic holiday crash.

Killer smog

All over the world people connect "London" with "fog", happily ignoring the fact that the Clean Air Act, restricting the use of some types of fuel, has made fog almost a rarity. It was very different in the old days when "pea-soupers" were part of every winter, but even hardened Londoners had never seen anything like the one that came down at the beginning of December 1952. At first it was just a nuisance, and they waited for the wind to blow it away. But no wind came, and the chimneys went on pouring dirt into the heavy air.

The city simply ground to a stop. People literally choked to death in their homes or in the streets. In the docks people fell into the river. Houses burned down before any fire engine could crawl to them, and sick people died long before an ambulance could reach them. Railway timetables became a farce, bus drivers got out and told their passengers they couldn't move another inch, and prize cattle at the Smithfield Show died in their stalls.

Birds crashed into buildings they couldn't see – one man was stunned by a low-flying mallard duck! Cinema managers suggested customers might like to check whether they could see the screen before they bought a ticket. Drivers gave up and left their cars wherever they were, and other blindly crawling cars banged into them. Electricity supplies began to fail as supplies of coal dwindled.

It only lasted four days, but in that time the smog combined with the icy weather to kill 4,000 people, particularly little children, the elderly and anyone with a weak chest. It really was the smog to end smog, for it became tragically obvious something had to be done to prevent it ever happening again.

Manufacturing death

Bhopal gave us a glimpse of the monsters created by twentieth-century science. But what happened on December 3, 1984, happened to poor people in a poor country, and many in the West have already forgotten it.

The Union Carbide factory in the Indian city of Bhopal made pesticides, though few of the thousands who lived in the surrounding shanty slums, made of cardboard and straw, knew that. When sirens woke them at one o'clock in the morning, they didn't realize they should run for their lives.

A valve had burst from over-pressure, the safety systems failed, and a forty-five-tonne tank of methyl isocyanate sent out a deadly cloud over the town. (In Britain, tanks rarely hold more than one tonne.) Methyl isocyanate involves phosgene in its manufacture, the dreaded gas of the First World War.

Parents and children lost each other in the fleeing crowds: choking in the dark, eyes burning, run over in panic by cars and buses, no one could outpace the cloud. The final toll was about 3,000 dead, and at least half a million with injuries, blindness and recurring sickness that ruined their lives.

For days the town was like a horror movie: bloated cattle dead in the streets, the hospitals overflowing with people dying in agony, withered leaves covered in the white ash of endless crematorium fires, packs of dogs digging up fresh graves. People whose religion forbids burying more than one body at a time had to pile loved ones into mass graves.

Union officials at the factory had warned about safety standards for two years, but neither the company nor the local state government had done anything. Third World nations, desperate for industry, often give multi-national companies freedom from pollution laws, and Union Carbide (who invented the Ever Ready dry-cell battery) is one of America's oldest and most powerful multi-nationals.

Three years later the Indian government was still fighting Union Carbide for £1,800 million in compensation, and a judge ordered £150 million as an interim payment. The legal battle could last years, until the victims, uneducated and poor, are defeated by the mountain of claim forms – or are dead.

Children suffering from the effects of the poison on their skin

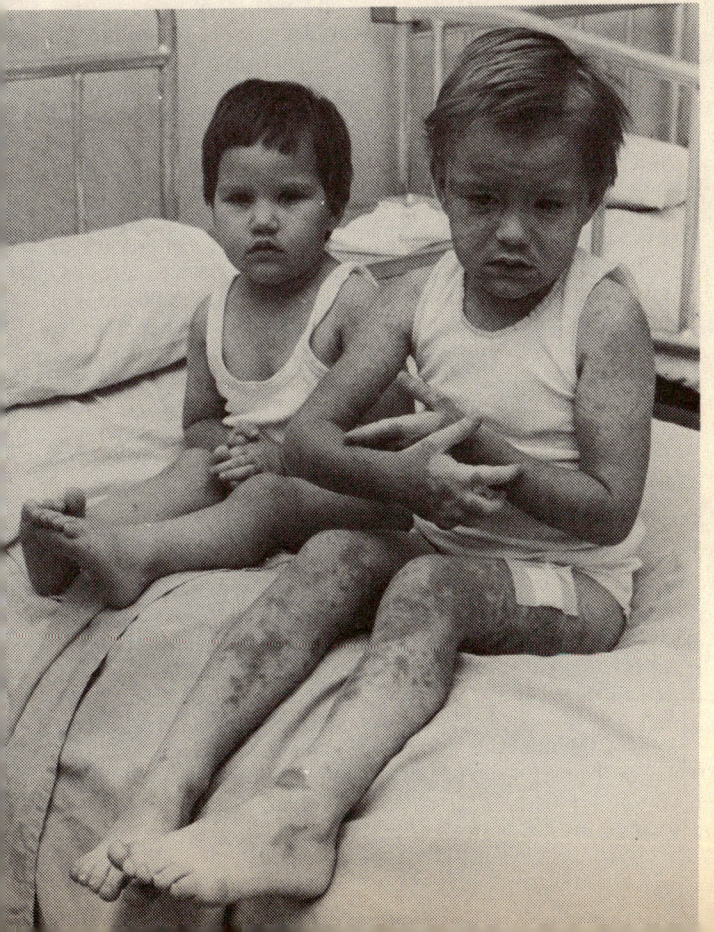

The world's worst fear come true

It was a confident group of highly skilled nuclear engineers who began the programme of tests on the Soviet RBMK boiling-water reactor at lunchtime on Friday, April 25, 1986, yet every move they made in the next twelve hours led them nearer to catastrophe.

The No. 4 reactor at Chernobyl – about 130 kilometres north of Kiev in the Ukraine – was shut down for the tests, but because the power was mistakenly allowed to fall below its stable point of twenty per cent, the operators' later mishandling led to an uncontrolled power surge. This disintegrated the nuclear fuel into fragments of white-hot ceramic, which reacted with boiling water to cause a violent steam explosion, cracking open the reactor. About thirty different fires created an inferno.

That night was young fire chief Leonid Teljatnikov's first major fire, but with suicidal courage he and his colleagues fought the fifteen-metre flames for three hours.

"It was our duty to other people," he said in hospital, knowing already he was going to die very soon from radiation.

The reactor spewed 100 million curies of radioactivity (one-tenth of the Nagasaki bomb) 1,500 metres into the sky, but though the core reached 2,000 degrees centigrade, its zirconium cladding saved it from meltdown, and helicopters were able to smother it with 5,000 tonnes of sand, clay and chemicals. Later 2,500 square kilometres of topsoil were removed and buried for ever.

The authorities either didn't realize or instinctively tried to hide the extent of the accident, and only high radioactivity recorded 1,500 kilometres away in Scandinavia told the world something was terribly wrong. The area was not evacuated for thirty-six hours, while the 40,000 inhabitants of the town of Chernobyl, sixteen kilometres away, remained for six days. The official Russian toll was thirty-

Soviet authorities check vehicles for radiation levels

one dead and 1,000 injured, with perhaps 6,530 dying from cancers in the next seventy years – foreign estimates range from 100,000 to 250,000 by critics of nuclear power.

We now know that every European government underestimated the radiation that was blown its way, perhaps to prevent panic. Hill farmers in Britain were told that there were no hazards at all to grazing sheep and cattle; then their animals were quarantined, and two years later, with grass radiation levels looking as if they will last into the next century, they knew their farms were dead.

The poison that can live forever

The people of Seveso, a northern suburb of industrial Milan, in Italy, are used to pollution, but even they knew the grey plume of smoke that exploded from the Icmesa factory smelled particularly choking and evil. It was lunchtime one July Saturday in 1976: outdoors in gardens or indoors in kitchens, everyone was affected.

At first the chemical company, a subsidiary of the Swiss drug firm Hoffman La Roche, denied anything more serious than a blown safety valve. By the fourth day pets and poultry had died; by the sixth, the first hospital case had been admitted and bewildered workers went on strike; next day came an official order to destroy all animals and plants in the immediate area.

Eight days after the accident the company admitted the cloud of trichlorophenol had contained dioxin, one of the most sinister poisons known to science.

Dioxin was used by the Americans to lay waste North Vietnam. Today we are beginning to realize the damage it did the Vietnamese people and the American and Australian troops, but its long-term effects are still a mystery. It is almost impossible to destroy. Previous accidents, in Germany, Holland, America and Britain, meant that just the factories had to be reduced to rubble, sealed and dumped in the sea or down a mineshaft: this time the poison had escaped over a whole district.

But all that the people of Seveso knew was that week by week more families were evacuated, and a thousand small animals and cattle died. Two years later hundreds of children still suffered the terrible effects on their skin.

Experts now believe the "danger zone" was both too small and wrongly mapped, that the poison was dispersed in the river, through vegetables, on car wheels and all the belongings of the fleeing people. The same government inefficiency that had allowed the company to bypass safety laws made a mess of coping with the resulting disaster.

Today this part of Seveso is dead – perhaps for ever.

People in neighbouring areas are so distressed they pretend it never happened. "All that fuss was just to get compensation," they say. They find that easier to live with than the thought of an unknown poisoned future.

The oil slick that threatens the world

Oil is the most widely scattered pollutant, floating in every corner of every sea, threatening all forms of life. Most of it is just leaked or thrown out, but every week, somewhere in the world, there are two potentially serious tanker accidents. Only the very worst make news.

1967 The 120,000-tonne *Torrey Canyon* hit the Seven Stones Reef, off Cornwall, in broad daylight and at full speed. She broke up and was eventually bombed to destroy the remaining oil, but not before 30,000 tonnes of it had ruined the coast and killed 25,000 birds.

1970 A 50,000-tonne Norwegian tanker ran aground and burst into flames in the Bay of Vigo, on the Spanish Atlantic coast. Her burning crude oil created a "firestorm" of black oily rain that even killed cattle and crops on shore. The crew were saved, but a fishing boat that went too near caught fire, killing everyone on board.

1978 A slick the size of Dorset – 223,000 tonnes of light crude oil – covered 220 kilometres of French coastline in Brittany and over 2,000 square kilometres of sea when the *Amoco Cadiz* lost her steering, ran aground and broke up. Delay and confusion in the salvage and clean-up operations led in 1984 to the biggest-ever marine pollution damage claim – $700,000,000 against the Indiana Standard Oil company.

1979 While the 62,000-tonne *Betelgeuse* was unloading in Bantry Bay, Ireland, she caught fire and exploded, killing fifty men. Not only did the death toll make this one of the worst disasters in the industry's history, but so did revelations that the ship's French owners, Total Oil, and the terminal operators, Gulf Oil, were slackly ineffici-

ent and deliberately saved money by neglecting safety. In 1982 four men were charged with perjury, having tried to cover up what really happened that night.

1984 The British tanker *Alvenus* ran aground and spilled 6,800,000 litres of crude oil from her ruptured tanks on 150 kilometres of Texan coast in the Gulf of Mexico.

1986 In another instance of delay and confusion, the bulk carrier *Kowloon Bridge* was allowed to return to sea, storm-damaged and against advice, only to be abandoned in a gale off south-west Ireland. She was left with engines running and turning in circles for thirty-six hours before sinking – and then allowed, over three months, to slowly release 1,200 tonnes of her bunker fuel. This is a persistent oil, difficult to disperse, and caused an *Amoco Cadiz*-type disaster which, perhaps because it was in slow motion, the rest of the world ignored.

1988 The Persian Gulf, gateway to so many oil-producing countries, is shallow, almost land-locked and has little intake of fresh water, so it's not surprising that it has forty-seven times the average pollution in proportion to its size. But the years of war between Iraq and Iran, and the mines laid in the Gulf waters, have endangered its very life.

The night the dam burst

The Vaiont Dam was the third highest in the world, and it haunted the thoughts of the Italian villagers who lived below it in little scattered communities – only the biggest, Longarone, is marked on a tourist road map. The authorities, however, were proud of this 280-metre high source of hydro-electric power, perched above an alpine valley in north-east Italy, where the Piave river runs on its way to the sea near Venice. They were not disturbed by reports that the mountain near it tended to crumble, and that a rock-slide into the dammed lake could cause a disaster.

Only three years after it was built, the disaster happened. At eleven o'clock on a wet and windy night in October 1963, a great chunk of mountain slid down into the water, sending a gigantic wave thundering over the edge of the dam into the valley below. When it hit the valley floor it reared up into a wall of water about 180 metres high, which roared down the valley smashing everything and everyone in its path – over 2,000 people, including 300 children.

Two years later an earthwork dam was built about sixty kilometres away across the Dolomite Mountains to the west, between Cavalese and Predazzo, to filter waste water from a fluorite mine. One July day in 1985 it gave way after heavy rains, and in twenty seconds hurled 250,000 cubic metres of water and mining sediment down the valley to the resort of Stava, burying villagers and holidaymakers in their chalets and hotel dining-rooms. The wall of water and debris, forty-five metres wide and almost as high, swallowed 269 people.

34

Drowning in sorrow

"With a poor woman like me, what is the point of living, of having to go through all this again and again?" This is the heartbreak of one survivor of the floods which devastated Bangladesh in 1987, as that tragic country struggles from one disaster to the next.

The Mouth of the Ganges, a vast flat area dotted with islands hardly higher than sandbanks, where thousands live in bamboo and thatch huts on stilts, is where two mighty rivers, the Ganges and the Brahmaputra, and their dozens of distributaries empty into the Bay of Bengal. In that part of the world hurricanes are called "cyclones", and, because the Bay of Bengal is shallow and narrows to the north, a cyclone sweeping up it creates a catastrophic tidal bore of water that has nowhere to go but over the land. In addition, cutting down the mountain forests has allowed billions of tonnes of silt to wash into the rivers, whose depth has fallen from sixty metres to twelve, till they overflow with the melting Himalayan snows and monsoon rains.

It is relentless: there have been eighteen major hurricanes since 1960. The water sweeps away everything – food, cattle, homes, clean

water – so destitute survivors face starvation, disease and exposure: one man clung to his wooden bed for forty-eight hours before a ship picked him up thirty kilometres out to sea.

A cyclone in 1985 killed 11,000 people and made 250,000 homeless; flooding in 1974 claimed at least 40,000 lives; in 1970 water and winds of 215 kph swept away *one million* people. That is so huge a number that the people become a mere statistic, and it is hard to think of them as suffering individuals, or the grief of those who were left.

Yet the severe 1987 floods, though they made a million homeless, killed "only" 1,400 – there was better organization, communications and health care, and government, army and voluntary grass-roots agencies combined resources. That may not have saved the rice crop, nor the roads, nor staved off disease, but it offers a ray of hope for the poor woman who wept but had to go on living.

Storm surge

When a giant wave buckled the loading doors of the *Princess Victoria* car ferry, on her way from Stranraer, Scotland, to Larne in Northern Ireland, she heeled over with the uneven weight of invading water, losing most of her lifeboats. Only two were left, and the women and children were put into one. But another wave upturned it, and every single one was drowned.

The 133 passengers and crew lost from the ferry were only the start of that weekend's death toll. It was Saturday, January 31, 1953, a time of full moon and high spring tides. And of a wind that reached force 11 – whole gale, and only one point from hurricane. It was cold with snow flurries.

The gale swept a mighty surge of water down the narrowing channel of the North Sea, over the coastal areas of eastern England, Holland and Belgium. It was not the creeping flood of a slowly rising river: it was, in most instances, a wall of sea-water bursting through the storm and killing people within seconds. Others died of injuries and cold in the swirling water, or from the effects of being trapped for days on a roof-top above the wintry sea.

In Holland, in spite of

centuries of experience in fighting back the sea, 1,785 people died and 100,000 were made homeless. More than a tenth of the farming and gardening land was flooded – 2,020 square kilometres.

In England 307 people died – mainly in Essex, Norfolk, Lincolnshire and Suffolk. Among the many heroes of the floods were American servicemen, two of whom received the George Medal for bravery, and seventeen Americans were among the dead. A vast quantity of livestock was drowned, and 25,000 homes flooded in up to six metres of water.

When the world showed it cared

Twice television pictures of starving children in Ethiopia have stung the world into action. In 1973 a documentary by Jonathan Dimbleby, shown in ten countries, told how 200,000 people had starved to death in nine months. Then in 1984 Michael Buerk presented a news report on an apparently unnoticed catastrophe – and prompted the biggest public appeal of all time.

This was a famine that had been known for a year, but no television station in America or Britain had thought it interesting enough to make news. By the time we see those haunting images on the screen it is always too late: all we can hope is to stop it happening yet again.

A one-time pop star, Bob Geldof, saw that programme, and decided tears and pity were no longer enough – it was time ordinary people did something, since it seemed governments were never going to. The astonishing efforts of this one man not only raised a vast sum of money but shamed governments into action by proving people do care about their fellow humans, no matter where they live.

First, he brought together British pop musicians – Band Aid – to raise £8,000,000 with a Christmas record; inspired by this, he organized a gigantic concert – Live Aid – linking Britain and America through television, and collected over £120 million. Soon everyone got the idea, and Sport Aid followed in 1986, with an unbelievable sixty million people worldwide running in a "Race Against Time" to feed the world.

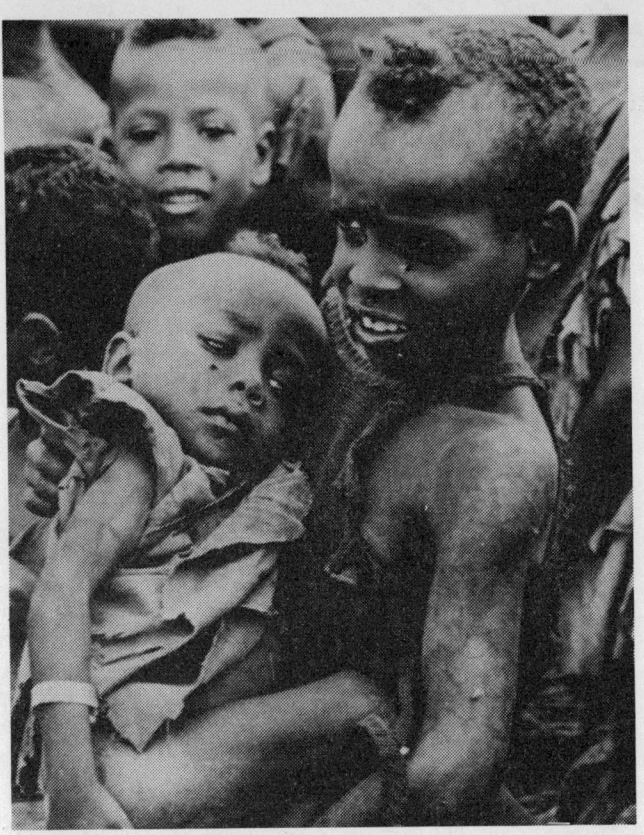

In 1984–5 there were ten million starving in Ethiopia, and one million of them died. But Geldof's organizational drive and initiative provided a valuable base for the future, with transport lorries, tools, seed, medical supplies, vermin-proof grain stores and dams – though food is needed immediately, it is essential to help a country feed itself.

The future is still bleak in many African nations. Another drought-stricken harvest and a seemingly endless civil war meant that in 1988 Ethiopia was facing famine again – and once more babies were dying on our television screens.

What's an earthquake really like?

There are up to half a million earthquakes happening each year, most of them too small to notice.

The *Mercalli* scale measures how it feels and what happens at any one place in an earthquake whereas the *Richter* scale measures the actual size of an earthquake in terms of its greatness (as seen on seismographs) related to the energy it is releasing. Earthquakes today are usually measured on the Richter scale. This is open-ended, and progresses logarithmically on a base of ten: 7.1 is ten times greater than 6.1, and 100 times worse than 5.1, and so on.

Richter	Mercalli	How it feels
Below 3.5	I	Only seismographs notice it
3.5	II	Might feel it if lying in bed, particularly in high buildings
4.2	III	Noticeable indoors, especially high up, rather like a light truck passing. Probably not recognizable as an earthquake
4.5	IV	House shudders or jolts, parked cars rock, glasses and crockery rattle, walls creak
4.8	V	Definitely an earthquake, recognizable outdoors. Might wake you up, doors swing, small objects fall over, windows and crockery might break
5.4	VI	Frightening, hard to walk. Furniture moves, tiles fall, bells ring, trees shake, windows break
6.1	VII	Everyone tries to run outdoors. Hard to stand. Furniture broken, walls crack or crumble. Poorly built homes on bad sites suffer severely. Noticeable even in a fast-moving car
6.5	VIII	Begin to panic. Can't steer cars, temperature and flow of springs and wells changes, wet ground cracks, all windows fall out, all buildings damaged, though slight in specially designed ones.
6.9	IX	General panic. All buildings damaged or collapse, underground pipes broken, noticeable cracks in the ground
7.3	X	Most buildings and their foundations destroyed. Large landslides, water slops on to banks of rivers and lakes, railways slightly bent, dams break
8.1	XI	Hardly any buildings remain. Landslides and floods sweep into valleys, railways bent like snakes.
Above 8.1	XII	Catastrophe. Total destruction of cities, ground moves in great waves. Uncontrollable panic and despair effects everyone.

1976: the year the earth shook

Every year there are dozens of earthquakes all over the world, each one at the very least unnerving if not reaching the tragic proportions that would take it into the news. If no one is killed, then the rest of the world hardly notices, but for those who have perhaps lost their home it is shattering.

Many earthquakes go far, far beyond that. 1976 was a year that brought an unusual number of severe quakes, with an appalling toll on man and his buildings.

In February, Guatemala, in Central America, suffered an earthquake that killed around 25,000 people, injured hundreds of thousands and destroyed property worth about $6,000,000,000.

May brought an earthquake to Udine, north-east Italy, which killed 1,000 people.

At the end of July northern China was struck by an absolutely devastating earthquake – quite how terrible no one knew at the time, for their government proudly and stubbornly refused to reveal the losses. But Tangshan, an industrial city of 1,000,000 people about 160 kilometres south-east of Beijing, was completely devastated, and Beijing itself and Tientsin, a major city to the south-west of Tangshan, were badly damaged. Later the world learnt that 650,000 people had lost their lives – a number of almost unbelievable horror.

In August a major earthquake, followed by an even greater disaster, a 15-metre *tsunami* (a "tidal wave" caused by underwater earthquakes), struck the southern Philippines, killing 8,000 and making over 50,000 homeless.

In September, Udine in Italy was struck again, terrifying the already frightened community and ruining earlier rebuilding, and Turkey, age-old earthquake victim, lost between 4,000 and 10,000 people and 200,000 homes in one hundred destroyed villages.

1976: a year to remember.

The hills ran and the sea disappeared

In May 1960 one of the greatest earthquakes ever recorded struck Chile, that immensely long narrow country running down the southern half of South America's west coast. In one sense it went on for weeks, with foreshocks and aftershocks, some of them almost as great as the main earthquake itself, which registered 8.7 on the Richter scale.

Inland, monstrous landslides devastated the countryside, whole mountains disappeared and people spoke of the "running hills". On the coast it was the dreaded tidal waves associated with earthquakes, the *tsunamis*, that were the destroyers. Chile has lived through many earthquakes, and when people saw the sea rise and suddenly draw back very fast, they were wise enough to run to the hills.

Corral is 16 kilometres from Valdivia – only a little port but you can find it marked on an atlas. After the first violent choppiness that followed the main shock, the sea rose, smoothly and fast, about five metres, flooding the town for about five minutes. Then with a sucking noise that must have been horrifying to hear, it rushed away, carrying one 3,000-tonne ship right over the harbour mole.

Sadly, the men of the town thought they had a chance at that point of saving some of their belongings and they ran down from the hill outside town. They were inevitably caught ten minutes later by the eight-metre-high *tsunami* that roared into the town at 200 kph, completely destroying everything. The women and children on the hill could only watch as the smashed remains of their houses and menfolk piled up together. The sea sucked itself out again.

An hour later, a much higher wave came in at about 95 kph, but by that time there was nothing left to destroy.

Along that whole coastal region, a stretch of land 29 kilometres wide and 483 kilometres long had sunk one-and-a-half to three metres in ten seconds. One writer, trying to bring the scale of this nearer home to us, points out that this is as if a great strip of land had sunk between Glasgow and Oxford, or between Canberra and Melbourne, or Memphis and New Orleans. For the Chileans as well as us, for such a thing to happen is almost unimaginable.

The city that roasted

Japan knows all about earthquakes from centuries of tragic experience. But Tokyo's earthquake of September 1, 1923 brought with it such destruction of life and property that it will never be forgotten.

For six hours there was a tremor every two minutes. The first shock came just before midday, when most families were preparing meals, and everywhere on that fiercely hot day stoves fell over and began disastrous fires. Later, whirlwinds sprang up in the furnace that the city had become and the whole area became an inferno. The meteorological office – before it burned down – recorded a temperature of 46°C and gusts of wind reached hurricane force of 240 kph. Densely packed crowds of fleeing people were roasted to death as they crowded into spaces they hoped would be safe.

Forty-eight kilometres away, Yokohama, Japan's most important port, was fighting a similar disaster. Some people were rescued by foreign ships and liners, but

the hurricane-force winds, the huge waves (not to mention the *tsunami* that followed the earthquake) and the ferocity of the flames made it a heroic and almost impossible job. Like Tokyo, Yokohama was pretty well wiped off the map. In one place the seabed itself sank 412 metres!

The fires raged for forty-six hours, and were of course followed by all the problems of no food and no medicines. By the end of it, 142,807 people had been killed, and those who were left, grieving, homeless and hungry, had scarcely the will to go on living.

Waking to a nightmare

"If you make a fist and run it under the blanket on your bed, the earth looked like the rippling on the blanket." There was a terrible booming noise, and **"buildings crumbled, really pancaked. Mexico has been hit with the force of a mighty blow from hell."**

These American visitors had been caught in the earthquake that shattered 791,000 square kilometres of southwest Mexico, coast to coast, at 7.20 in the morning of September 19, 1985. In three minutes, the 8.1 force devastated the centre of Mexico City, but with the epicentre 400 kilometres away in the Pacific ocean, the western coastal states bore the brunt and dozens of ships were lost in a sea that boiled up into twenty-two-metre waves.

The press created one symbol of hope. Although 200 newborn babies died in the rubble of the city's hospitals, fourteen were dug out after several days and survived, the heat and moist concrete acting like incubators! International rescue teams rushed to Mexico, but, like many poor and politically nervous countries, the death toll given by the government of 4,200 was ludicrously low. Experts agree 45,000 is nearer the truth, and two years later there were still thousands of homeless protesting about lack of help.

In the sensation of a disaster, we sometimes forget the effect, for years after, on survivors. Doctors in Mexico City have reported on the insomnia and nightmares, the depression, madness and suicides (many unable to face being crippled) that the earthquake triggered. Over and over, people were panicked by the illusion, called "Phantom Quake", that the ground was moving under them again. Some survivors seemed quite undisturbed simply because they would not, could not, believe their families had gone: like the volunteers who toiled so sturdily in the rescue, their mental collapse, when it did arrive, was even worse.

The fiercest eartl

On Good Friday, 1964, southern Alaska suffered one of the
most powerful earthquakes the
world has known in modern
times. It registered 8.6 on the
Richter scale, that is greater
than the famous San Francisco
earthquake of 1901. (Only the
very largest quakes exceed
8.4, and the energy they
release is about one hundred
times greater than that of
the atom bomb dropped on
Hiroshima.)

Over the whole of Alaska
about 200,000 square kilometres of land was lifted up or
dropped by at least a metre,
and the great sea waves it
caused wrecked towns and
killed people along the coast
as far south as California.
Inland lakes as far away as
Florida – way over in the
south-east of the USA – were
sloshed about by the seismic
waves.

Houses, cars, trees and

people tumbled into deep chasms in and around Anchorage, 160 kilometres from the earthquake centre, and a prosperous suburb overlooking Cook Inlet slid down a collapsing cliff 470 metres to the sea.

The death toll, of about 200, was not as heavy as it might have been if the area had been a more thickly populated one, but for those who lived through it the experience was devastating. In Valdez, eighty kilometres from the earthquake centre, the sea sucked away from the pier and docks where thirty men, women and children were waiting for a boat, and then roared back in an eight-metre-high wave that smashed everything in its path. Ten minutes later a second great surge of water, this time laden with massive debris, rushed in.

The liner that sank in fourteen minutes

Within three years three mighty transatlantic liners sank, each one taking over 1,000 people to the bottom with her, and each – it seems, with hindsight – needlessly: The *Titanic* in 1912, the *Lusitania* in 1915, and, in between and almost forgotten, the *Empress of Ireland* in May, 1914.

The *Titanic* drowned the darlings of rich society, the *Lusitania* was torpedoed by a ruthless enemy – an act which brought America into the First World War – but the *Empress of Ireland* was filled only with ordinary middle-class people and immigrant working families: momentarily, the world was saddened by the size of the death-roll, but soon passed on to weightier matters.

She was on her first night

out from Quebec, sailing slowly down the St Lawrence Seaway, infamous for its peculiarities of depth and fog. Her captain, Kendall, was the man who had first used radio to capture a criminal – the murderer Crippen. After the *Titanic* disaster, she was packed with more than enough lifeboats.

But when, at 1.30 a.m. in a sudden bank of fog, the reinforced steel hull of a Norwegian collier, the *Storstad*, sliced into the liner like a great chisel below her waterline, the monstrous hole allowed 273,000 litres of water a second to pour into both boiler-rooms. As she listed, the portholes that lined every great ship of those days also came under the water and caved in.

It had been a gentle collision that most of the passengers had never even noticed but within only fourteen minutes the liner had slipped beneath the water – far too fast to rescue many passengers who were still unfamiliar with the ship's layout. One thousand and twelve people drowned, either trapped in the liner, or after a few moments in water so icy it killed even those in lifejackets.

Each captain and crew was honest and experienced. Each accused the other of changing course in the fog. Each swore they saw the other's lights in positions that justified their own actions. A commission blamed the *Storstad*, but how the collision happened will never really be explained.

North Sea turnover

Outside, the March weather was dreadful – winds of 130 kmh whipping up huge waves – but inside the oil rig the men were snug, waiting for the start of the evening film, or resting on their bunks.

By 1980 the four-year-old *Alexander Kielland* had been converted from a drilling rig to an accommodation platform – a "flotel" – for workers on the next-door *Edda* rig. But its 200-tonne derrick had been left on the platform (making it top-heavy), and, unlike drilling rigs, which are allowed to up anchor and drift with the swell in heavy seas, it was anchored permanently to the *Edda*.

The 10,105-tonne Norwegian rig was home for 213 men working in the Ekofisk oil field, 265 kilometres off Stavanger, Norway, far into the North Sea. That stormy night there were two bumps, a crack, and suddenly lights went out, alarms sounded and everything was flung about as the rig tilted at forty-five degrees. Radio messages called all shipping to the rescue, but within fifteen minutes this monster, the size of the Albert Hall, was hanging upside down.

The off-duty workers were not wearing survival clothing,

so the icy sea, just above freezing, meant death within minutes. By morning it was clear that 123 men, many from Britain, were lost.

The inquiry revealed some ruthless facts. Basic design faults plus shoddy welding had caused the fifth leg to break under stress ten metres below the water line. The whole design, with its cylinders of thin steel (derived from the *aerospace* industry), had never been properly researched for metal fatigue or for the random forces of the sea, and tests on five other oil rigs showed they, too, were just as dangerous.

The secret of the sea-bed

The nuclear submarine USS *Thresher* was designed to cruise at 300 metres. Below that, depending how deep she went, colossal underwater pressure would damage her and eventually cause her to collapse.

One morning in April 1963 she was doing a routine deep dive in the Atlantic, about 320 kilometres off Cape Cod. With her was a submarine rescue vessel, the *Skylark*. The sea at that point is over 2,500 metres deep.

After ninety minutes the *Skylark* received a message from the *Thresher* that they were dealing with a minor problem. Then there was silence. "Are you in control? Are you in control?" repeated the *Skylark*. Another silence. Followed by a blurred message, hard to distinguish, something about "set depth" – it might have been "exceeding set depth". Then sounds of the submarine breaking up. After that, only an unbroken silence.

A court of inquiry thought

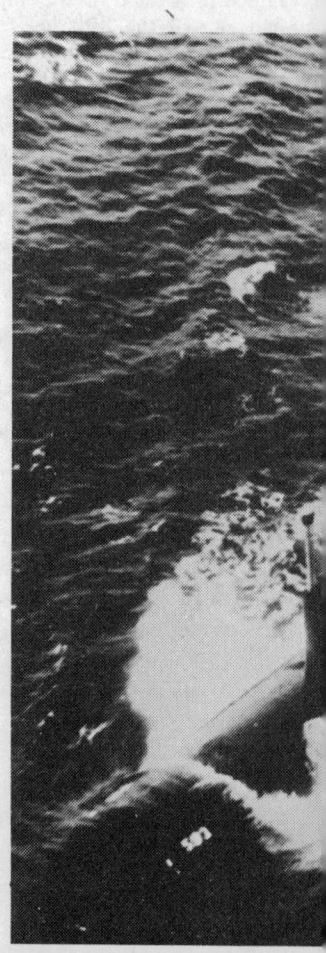

a salt-water piping system in the engine room had probably failed, and anything that brought water flooding in would have caused the *Thresher* to fall rapidly beyond her safe level. But what really happened to her and the crew of 129 men who sank with her will always be a mystery.

Death the ferryman

Crossing the English Channel by ferry is such a familiar routine that no one could believe the unthinkable had happened when the *Herald of Free Enterprise*, on its way to Dover, capsized outside the Belgian harbour of Zeebrugge, in March 1987.

It seems the ferry company was lulled into the same complacency – in spite of research showing there had been 1,352 serious accidents in these northern waters in just five years, 1978–83. Intent on cutting costs and speeding up schedules, it, like others, ignored safety warnings and earlier lessons and allowed, an inquiry was told, "a sloppy system" to develop.

It had become a habit to set out with the bow (front) doors still open, so that when the *Herald of Free Enterprise*, which was known to list to the side anyway, was weighed down with a heavy load and too many passengers, she ploughed through her own bow wave, flooded the car decks and within minutes turned over.

The basic danger in the design of "roll-on roll-off" ferries combined with human carelessness to kill 193 people, including complete families. And a year later, the corroded drums of lethal chemicals that had ben illegally on board were still awaiting safe disposal.

This disaster haunts Britain, but it pales beside the loss of life later that year when the passenger ship *Dona Paz* collided with a small oil tanker just before Christmas. She was grossly overcrowded with people going to join families in Manila, the capital of the Philippines, the great chain of western Pacific islands. Blazing from the exploding oil, they both sank in a burning sea in the straits off Mindoro, 180 kilometres south of Manila.

It's a story of negligence and corruption: the tanker was operating illegally, both their radio licences had expired so they couldn't send an SOS, they lacked lifejackets and lifeboats, and rescue was hopelessly slow. No one knows how many were on board, but at least 2,000 died – only twenty-six people were saved.

It was the worst sea disaster in peacetime – worse than the sinking of the *Titanic*.

Pearl Harbor: sitting target

In 1941 Japan was intent on expanding her own empire in the Pacific and China. General Tojo had become the Japanese Prime Minister, and he was determined to speed up Japan's successes by military force in a way he knew that America would not tolerate. Until then the United States, anxious not to be involved in a foreign conflict, had tried to

negotiate with Japan. Surprise, then, was Japan's secret weapon.

Both sides were still negotiating on the morning of December 7, when news of the Japanese attack on Pearl Harbor broke. The Americans had been fairly successful at decoding Japanese secret messages, but they hadn't realized that Japan had managed to get their aircraft carriers within striking distance of Hawaii, where ninety-four ships of the American Navy were anchored.

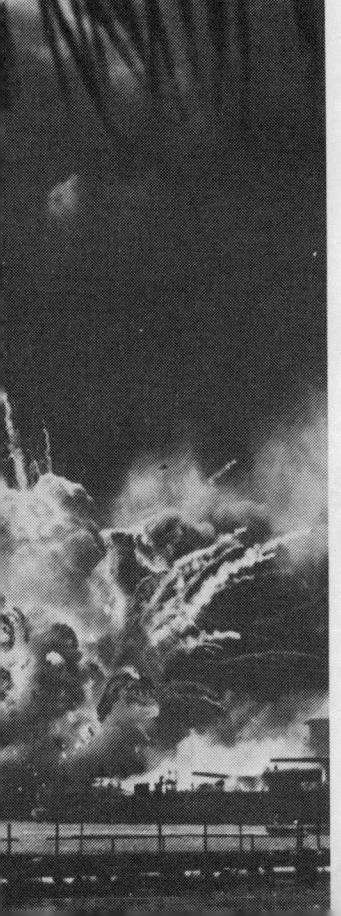

Just before eight o'clock the first wave of Japanese dive bombers came over the unsuspecting base. Two hours later all America's Pacific naval power lay in smoking ruins. Four great battleships were sunk, and fifteen other ships were either sunk or badly damaged. Over 3,000 servicemen were dead – without having even gone to war.

All America was stunned, and then enraged. Throughout the rest of the war several individual officials were savagely accused in the nation's search for someone to blame. In truth, the disaster had come from a combination of slow reactions and errors of judgement in various departments, and the fact that the fleet should perhaps have never been sent, in over-confidence, so far from home support.

It was a turning-point for America and for the world. That night President Roosevelt phoned Prime Minister Churchill in England. "We are all in the same boat now," he said. The United States had declared war. And that was to prove a disaster for Japan.

Gallipoli: murder or suicide?

The First World War was, you could say, one big disaster after another. But the bitterness of the Gallipoli campaign has lingered for generations.

At the time no one could understand why men were fighting 5,600 kilometres away when the real war was being slogged out just across the Channel. They couldn't understand that to reach Constantinople (now Istanbul) would divert the enemy and end the horrifying slaughter in the trenches. But the plan at headquarters was half-hearted, orders arrived late, and ammunition was ruthlessly held back – in spite of its colossal waste every day in France to gain absolutely no ground at all.

The Gallipoli peninsula is eight kilometres wide at its narrowest point. In 1915 the Allied army tried to cross it after the Navy had failed to get through the minefield at the entrance to the Dardanelles. The Australian and New Zealand Army Corps bore the brunt of the campaign – the Anzac landing was named after them. One Australian brigade of 2,000, charging to the cry, "Come on, Australia!", lost over 1,000 men in half-an-hour.

Heat and a crippling lack of water added to the misery

and losses, and a sense of being cut off from all comfort, with only the sea at their backs, lowered the men's spirits. The Turks' fierce resistance was resented at first – until someone pointed out that the place did belong to them. The soldiers later came to have respect and admiration for the Turks' attitude, which was dogged and defiant instead of the easily bribed cowardice that the British generals had predicted.

To push through those eight kilometres the allies flung half-a-million men on the Peninsula – and lost over 250,000 of them.

After eight months nothing at all had been gained, except an orderly retreat. All that was left is a memory of the men from all over the French and British Empires, and particularly the Anzacs, who never refused an order, no matter how suicidal.

Mighty *Hood's* last battle

By the time the Second World War broke out, HMS *Hood* was really out of her time. She had been built at the end of the previous war, and it was only Britain's great need, and a hasty refit, that sent her out to fight again.

To the country at large, however, she was reckoned the mighty ship she had always been – no one was told of Germany's powerful navy, and certainly nothing about the superiority of such battle-

ships as the *Bismarck*. To Britain, *Hood* was the finest ship afloat – "the mighty Hood". People forgot she was a battle-cruiser, not a battleship.

When word came that *Bismarck* had been sighted south of Bergen, Norway, in May 1941, *Hood* and the *Prince of Wales* set out to prevent the *Bismarck* from reaching the Atlantic at all costs. Both navies were confident, but the only advantage the British actually had was their radar, and the fact that *Bismarck* didn't realize that *Hood* and *Prince of Wales* were after her.

When they met, everything was on the Germans' side – their better gunnery equipment, the angle of approach, and the weather. Both *Bismarck* and *Hood* were hit, but within minutes a column of flame shot into the sky from *Hood*'s centre section: she had been hit in one magazine which had blown up another, and within moments she keeled over and sank. Over 1,400 men went down with her.

The searching destroyers found only three survivors, a patch of oil and a few bits of wood – all that was left of the pride of the Royal Navy. The naval commanders in London, and the rest of the fleet, were stunned. The Germans were broadcasting the news in triumph, so it had to be released to the BBC and the newspapers. The country simply couldn't believe it, and only the thought of hunting the *Bismarck*, and this time annihilating her, gave any comfort at all. And indeed, only a few days later, the *Bismarck* was sunk by HMS *Dorsetshire* to the west of Brest, in France, on May 27, 1941.

HMS *Hood* leaving Plymouth.

65

The hero of the Christmas express

It was late on Christmas Eve 1953 in New Zealand. Everywhere people were travelling home for family reunions, looking forward to the food and presents next day.

The tallest mountain on New Zealand's North Island is an active volcano, Mount Ruahepu, with a crater lake that every so often becomes hot and sulphurous from the eruptions beneath it. After an eruption in 1948 the outlet from the lake had become blocked with debris and ice so that its level built up dangerously.

On this Christmas Eve night just a small rise in volcanic activity caused the water of the lake to burst through its barrier, sending about 2,700 million litres of hot acid water, mixed with mountain debris, ash and mud, thundering into the Whangaehu River. The lake had fallen by nine metres and the river became unrecognizably murderous.

A young postal worker called Ellis was driving home for Christmas with his wife and mother-in-law when he came to a bridge across the Whangaehu. The water was already threatening the road and, although it was hard to see in the dark, he guessed the railway bridge would never support a train.

At that moment, over the noise of the wind, they heard a train approaching – the Wellington express, packed with holiday-makers on their way to Auckland. Young Ellis ran back along the track and tried desperately to warn the express with his torch. But there was not nearly enough time for such a fast train to pull up, and the engine and first five coaches plunged into the boiling river.

The sixth coach still hung on the edge, and Ellis struggled into it shouting to people to jump out while they could. But suddenly it too crashed into the river – taking him with it. One hundred and fifty-one people died in this, one of the country's worst accidents. Yet, incredibly, not only did Ellis manage to escape but he helped many others to, as well. He was later awarded the George Medal for his bravery.

But that Christmas morning, instead of the usual cheerful programmes, all over New Zealand people listened to a national announcement on their radios of loved ones killed or missing.

Traffic falls on train

The rush-hour express was full of schoolchildren and city workers as it came through Granville, a suburb of Sydney, Australia, on the morning of January 18, 1977. It had come from the Blue Mountains, just to the west of Sydney, and it was heading for the worst rail accident Australia has ever suffered.

What happened sounds frighteningly simple. One young man said afterwards, "The train took a bend near the bridge too fast and tipped over." It crashed into one of the overhead bridge supports, and the bridge and its traffic smashed down on to the train, squashing two of the carriages to about one metre from the ground.

Rescuing the 200 trapped passengers was dreadfully complicated: there was the wreckage from the falling cars, and the train had not only broken a 1500-volt overhead power line but had also damaged a gas main, so that rescuers dared not use cutting torches for fear of an explosion. Cranes had to try to lift the bridge off the carriages in whole sections, and in the end eighty people died.

The ship at the end of the road

In 1980, within the space of a few months, two Liberian-registered cargo ships on opposite sides of the world crashed into bridges, tumbling traffic into a nightmare darkness.

Heavy fog prevented cars seeing the Almoe Bridge being ripped away on the night of January 18, and they fell helplessly thirty-seven metres into the frozen waters of the Hake Fjord, near Gothenburg on Sweden's west coast. Fifteen people died.

Then on May 9 a second ship knocked out 400 metres of the four-lane highway on the Sunshine Skyway Bridge, a twenty-four-kilometre span over Tampa Bay at St Petersburg, Florida. A thunderstorm was raging over the morning rush-hour traffic: it was dark, windy and raining. A Greyhound bus, two cars and a lorry toppled forty-three metres below into the main shipping canal, killing over thirty people. One car slowed to a stop just on the edge, and its four passengers crawled to safety. "You could hear their screams above the storm," said an eyewitness.

Giant boxes, giant boxes

An absolute rash of disasters forced the world of engineering to think again about an experimental method of building bridges which had seemed both cheap and fast. The box girder system uses giant pre-fabricated boxes of steel joined to each other, and it is extremely difficult for engineers to work out the different points of strain and support on each box unit.

A bridge being built over the Danube in Vienna, Austria, collapsed in 1969, and in June 1970 a falling bridge at Milford Haven in Wales killed five workmen. Four months later one of the largest bridges in the world, across the River Yarra, near Melbourne, Australia, collapsed as it was being built. It happened while the engineers were trying to find out why two box girders had met with a 110 millimetre gap and why one of the sections had started to buckle. They laid eighty tonnes' worth of concrete blocks on one box to force it to meet the other, and undid the bolts on the buckled section in the hope it would straighten. But instead the buckle spread, and shortly afterwards the whole span collapsed, sending concrete blocks crashing down on to the workmen's huts. Thirty-five men died.

A year later a road bridge over the Rhine at Koblenz in Germany also collapsed while it was being built, and killed nine people. Engineers everywhere began re-examining their box girder bridges.

Challenger to the gods

"Feel that mother go ... Woo-hoo!" was the exultant cry of Challenger 7's pilot, Mike Smith, at the command to throttle up.

Seconds later the shuttle, symbol of American power and pride, exploded thirteen kilometres above the earth in a massive supersonic steam cloud. Millions across the world watching it on television, as well as friends and relatives at the launchpad, gazed in unbelieving horror.

Their disbelief arose from the same source as the tragedy. NASA (National Aeronautics and Space Administration) had come to believe they were infallible. Commercial pressure to show off to Congress and future customers had made them so ambitious that over the years they had dismantled safety and quality controls, played down problems, and created an overexcited hype linking Challenger's success to American patriotism.

Seven astronauts perished with Challenger 7, including a schoolteacher, Christa McAuliffe, on the team purely to demonstrate how safe and ordinary space travel had become.

January 28, 1986, the day of the launch at Florida's Kennedy Space Center, was cold, but having delayed already for five days, NASA decided to push ahead. The rubber seals of the solid-fuel rocket boosters had failed before, and the link with low temperatures was well known, yet the risk was taken – and, after a seventy-five-second flight, erupting fuel blasted the tank of pressurized liquid hydrogen.

The day before had been the nineteenth anniversary of the death of three top astronauts in the Apollo disaster, criticized for risking safety in the space race against Russia.

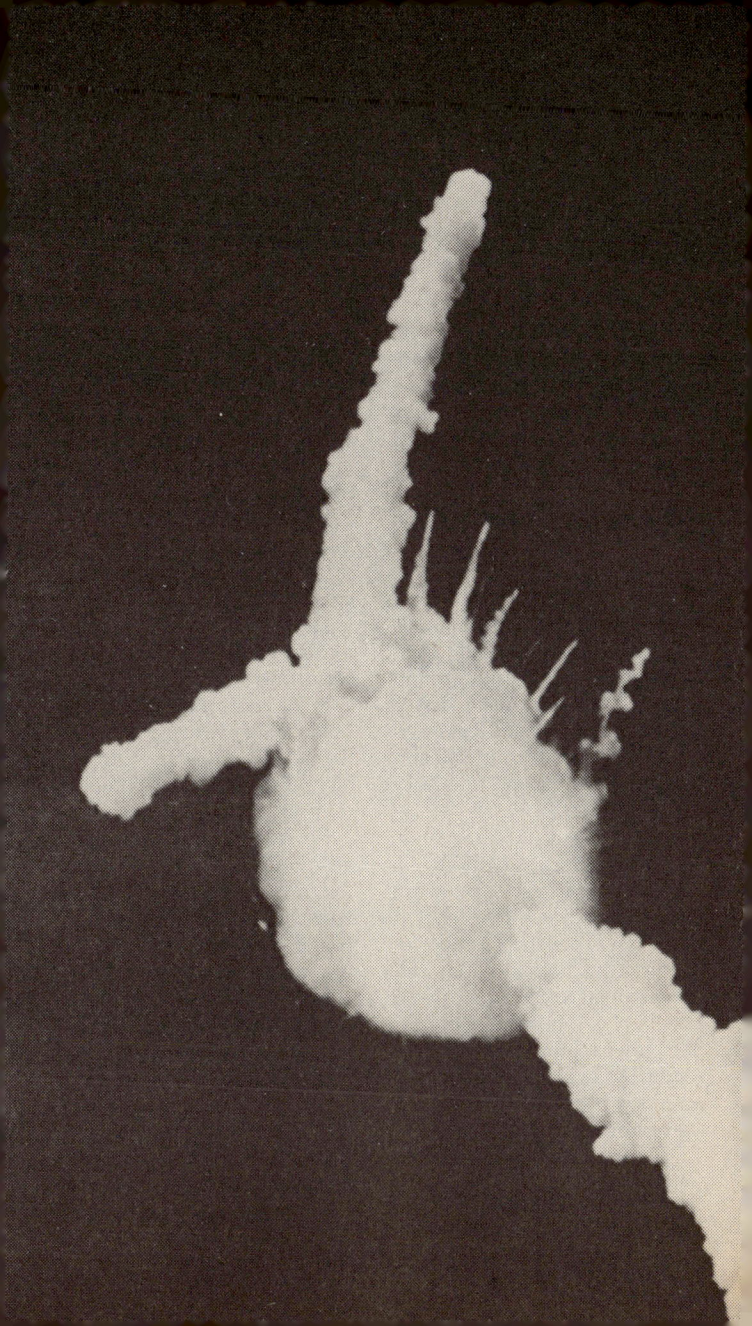

Near miss for mankind

An enormous object is hurtling towards the earth. As it enters the earth's atmosphere it glows more brightly than the early morning sun. It has crossed the Indian Ocean and is now over western China, approaching central Russia.

There people are terrified by a deafening roar, and a tremendously powerful blast of air pushes trees, animals and men to the ground. Then a vast area of Siberia, around the Stony Tunguska River right in the heart of Russia, is shaken by an absolutely cataclysmic explosion. It is 7.17 a.m.

Far away, earthquake tremors are recorded, in Irkutsk, Moscow, Jena in Germany, even in Washington and Java. At the moment of impact a nineteen-kilometre-high pillar of fire leaps into the sky and is seen by people in towns hundreds of kilometres away. For 800 kilometres people are frightened by thunderous explosions.

At the same time, a scorching wave of air sets the northern forests on fire – they will burn for days. A trading post sixty-four kilometres away is blasted by a shock wave that collapses houses and flings people unconscious into the air. At Kansk, 603 kilometres away, the railway and town are shaken by a series of shock waves that will circle the globe twice.

Dust and debris sucked into the vortex of the explosion form into thick clouds nineteen kilometres up and fall as "black rain". During the next nights the skies of Europe and north-east Asia will be lit by a luridly bright glow.

For forty-eight kilometres all round the point of impact the trees are burnt and blasted backwards like millions of spokes in a circle.

Is it a meteor? A comet? A collision between earth and a body of anti-matter?

All this happened on June 30, 1908, and because it took place in a remote part of the world, very hard to reach and dangerous to explore, and because Russia, heading for

revolution, had other things to worry about, it was many years before scientists began to investigate.

What is eerie to think about is how lucky the earth was: only reindeer, trees and birds were killed. But if the collision had happened only four hours later it would have hit Leningrad like several hydrogen bombs. If it had fallen in the sea (and seventy per cent of the earth is covered in water) it would have caused devastating tidal waves on every shore. If it had fallen on ice (and ten per cent of the earth is ice-covered) it would have melted enough great chunks to alter our sea level and climate.

Could it happen again? A Soviet scientist has announced that we are already on a collision course with a giant asteroid, calculated to hit the earth in 2115. This time mankind's best chance is to blow it up in space first.

Space's longest journey... to eternity

It looked as if the three Russian astronauts had been spectacularly successful. Vladislav Volkov, Viktor Patsayev and Georgi Dobrovolsky were re-entering earth's atmosphere in Soyuz II after the longest journey in space that man had ever made: 23 days, 17 hours, 41 minutes.

They had proved that it was possible to supply crews from earth to an unmanned space laboratory by docking Soyuz II with an orbiting space station, Salyut, and carrying out experiments there. (Patsayev had his thirty-eighth birthday up there, and his mates had smuggled an onion and a lemon on board as presents.)

Thirty minutes before landing, something happened that brought a rapid drop in pressure, and the three men died in the fifteen seconds it would take for their blood to boil in the vacuum. Long space flights do strange and unknown things to a man's mind and body, and it is possible that they were behaving less efficiently by the end of their long mission, and didn't close their hatch properly. Certainly, two days before their re-entry, their commander had radioed, "We have had enough."

The white mountain with the black soul

If you look at a map of South America, you'll see, just north of Lima, Peru, a town called Huaras. It is a resort of hot springs, one of many picturesque and colourful towns and villages in a spectacularly beautiful valley, the Callejón de Huaylas – sometimes called the Switzerland of South America. It is rich and fertile (it was here the Spaniards first came across the potato) and densely populated.

Completely dominating the valley is one of the highest mountains in the whole of the Andes, Mount Huascarán, which stands at 6,700 metres – far higher than Mont Blanc or the Matterhorn. It belongs to a chain of mountains on the eastern side of the valley that shine dazzlingly white and lovely, but whose near-vertical slopes regularly send down murderous avalanches. One, in 1962, sent over three million tonnes of Huascarán's northern peak hurtling down a drop of 3,960 metres, travelling fourteen kilometres in seven minutes, burying the village of Ranrahirca and killing 3,500 people.

The survivors managed to rebuild their village – but the mountain hadn't finished with them yet.

On May 30, 1970, a 13,000-square-kilometre area of Peru was shaken by a major earthquake centred under the seabed about twenty-four kilometres out from the port of Chimbote, a growing industrial city that is fed by power from a hydroelectric plant on the River Santa as it flows through the mountains on the western, coastal, side of the Callejón de Huaylas, this scenic valley. The earthquake registered 7.9 on the Richter scale, and within a 160-kilometre radius of Chimbote its side-to-side movements had a devastating effect on buildings.

In the coastal areas, the number of deaths was not unusually high, but inland, in the villages of the Callejón de Huaylas, it was as if the world had come to an end. In the pretty little town of Huaras, within forty-five seconds, over 16,000 people were buried among the ruins, and the story was repeated in all the small communities throughout the valley and its mountains. That was before Mount Huascarán joined in.

A slab of ice and rock nearly one kilometre wide – probably more than 1,000,000 cubic metres – broke off the mountain's northern peak. Gathering huge quantities of material as it slid down at speeds of up to 430 kph, travelling fourteen kilometres in under four minutes, it forked into three tongues: one wiped out several small villages, one buried the newly built Ranrahirca, leaving only fifty people alive, and one rushed on to the city of Yungay, which had been spared its neighbour's fate in 1962.

Yungay had been protected in the past from landslides by a ridge of about 200 metres high. But this 1970 monster simply reared up over the ridge, sending a massive wall of debris as high as a ten-storey building crashing over the city, burying it five metres deep. With it were buried 15,000 residents plus, because it was Sunday, thousands more who were visiting or getting ready for market day.

Flooding, and other smaller landslides, added to the toll. The mud dried hard like a layer of brick, ranging between twenty-five millimetres and nine metres thick. Everything in its path was totally devastated, and it was weeks before the situation could be properly assessed. Boulders of unbelievable size lay scattered through the once lovely valley: a 14,000-tonne rock (that's as heavy as 2,000 elephants) lay where Ranrahirca had been, and one of 7,000 tonnes at Yungay, along with thousands of smaller ones. Geologists reckoned later that the material moved by the avalanche had been more than a quarter the amount dug out to make the Panama Canal – and that had taken ten years.

In the end, the final toll of that tragic Sunday afternoon was 200,000 homeless, 50,000 injured, and 70,000 dead.

The village that lost its children

Steven Palmer's mother took him to the doctor one morning. While he was there the great coal tip that loomed above the village roared down on to his school. By eleven o'clock that morning he was the only one of his class left alive.

Aberfan. Even today the name of this little village in a

Welsh mining valley echoes with grief and horror for anyone old enough to remember October 21, 1966. At 9.15 that morning the dark, glistening tip of dense, semi-liquid waste, over 315 metres high, slipped as many had feared it would, and engulfed nineteen houses and Pantglas Junior School.

Five teachers and 116 children died, as well as twenty-three other men and women. The children were mostly aged between seven and ten – the disaster wiped out almost that whole age group in the village – and many of them were brothers and sisters.

A small, closely-knit, not very well-off village, Aberfan never recovered. The size of the world-wide relief fund left people confused and bewildered. So many mothers sent their children to school that morning never to see them again, so many fathers waited day and night to find and identify their own small boy or girl, that the shared sorrow was more than one village could cope with. Even the children who survived were scarred by fear and pathetic feelings of guilt for being alive when their friends were dead.

Many families thought of escaping from the valley with its black coal tips and starting a new life, but few could bring themselves to leave their children behind in the little hillside cemetery.

Now just a name on a map

"My husband was watching television right next to me," one woman wept, "and then I saw him swept away by the mud."

July of 1987 brought flood havoc (just as in 1983 and 1985) to a large area around Sondrio, near the Swiss border of Italy, washing away roads, railways, bridges and thousands of animals, bringing mudslides that cut houses in half and destroyed blocks of flats and a hotel at Tartano. Sixteen people, like that woman's poor husband, died, and many were trapped in their mud-spattered nightclothes on rooftops.

Italy's Lake District, near the Swiss border east of Lake Como, has a fragile natural balance that geologists say has been deliberately disturbed for the sake of the tourist and winter sports industries. Roads have been slashed through mountains, forest cut down, and a rash of unplanned building litters the valley slopes. But there is a price to pay.

Villages along the banks of the River Adda, which flows into Lake Como, were ordered to evacuate everybody except workmen, but some people slipped back illegally to their homes. This order saved a massive tragedy ten days later, when millions of cubic metres of mud and rock hurtled down a mountainside, burying three villages around Morignone – which you can now find only on a map. Twenty villagers and seven workmen disappeared under the devastation.

The world's worst train crashes

Two of the worst ever train accidents happened during the First World War, and involved troop trains, but so many millions were dying in that appalling war that the death roll of hundreds in a train crash – a number that would have stunned a peace-time world – was swallowed up by other horrors and almost forgotten.

In May 1915, a combination of laziness, bending the rules and sheer absent-mindedness on the part of two signalmen brought Quintinshill, near Gretna Green in Scotland, the worst train crash Britain has ever suffered.

A troop train with 500 men from the Royal Scots Regiment crashed into a waiting local train, and a minute later an express, cheerfully travelling at its usual speed, tore into the wreckage and survivors. The resulting fire was unquenchable.

Most of the 227 dead and 246 injured were soldiers. Both the signalmen were held responsible and imprisoned, but they each suffered nervous breakdowns and were freed after a year.

Two years later in France came the worst rail disaster the world has even seen. Two trains, absolutely crammed

with homeward-bound troops from Italy, were joined together. The driver complained that the ineffective hand brakes on most of the coaches would not face up to the steep slopes ahead as he crossed the Alps, but the train was already late and he was ordered to go ahead.

He had been right. As the overladen train went cautiously down the slope from Modane, in Savoie, it relentlessly picked up speed on the slippery, frosty line, until it was eventually quite out of control. The friction of the brake blocks set fire to the carriages – where soldiers were bringing back souvenir grenades and shells – and the blazing train jumped the rails into a high wall at over 145 kph.

Because of the wartime censor and identification difficulties no one knows the exact number who died, but 425 were named and it is thought that the total was between 550 and 800.

Silent horror

There is an eerie quietness about another wartime rail tragedy, one that happened in 1944 in the mountains of Basilicata in Italy. No crash, no wreckage, no noise at all . . .

The train was a goods train, but it was packed with illegal passengers, some local but many dodging the law and looking for a way over the mountains. With forty-seven wagons, it needed two engines, and even then it had

a tough job climbing with its load. Apparently the firemen had grumbled about the poor wartime coal, which seemed only good for making smoke. Whether from the extra weight or the useless coal, the train stopped just after entering an uphill mountain tunnel.

Perhaps the two drivers couldn't agree on what to do next, try to go on or go back, but before anything was decided the lethal carbon monoxide of the smoke in the tunnel had killed not only them and their firemen but the hundreds of passengers in the wagons behind.

Some, who were still in the open air at the back of the train, survived, but by the time rescue came, 509 people had silently died in one train standing all alone on a mountain.

The underground train that didn't stop

It is a reflection on the safety record of London's Underground system that the Moorgate station crash in February 1975 still seems, despite the horrific 1987 fire at King's Cross, quite unbelievable.

Why, no one will ever know, but the driver of a morning rush-hour train on the Highbury branch of the Northern Line made no attempt to slow down, far less stop, as he approached the dead-end wall at Moorgate underground station. Was he ill? Was he committing suicide and taking his passengers with him?

Whatever his reasons, the results were catastrophic. The front coaches concertinaed into the blind tunnel, and rescue workers took many,

many hours in appalling conditions to reach the dead and injured. Further down the train coaches had mounted and crushed each other.

Seventy-four people were injured, and forty-two died that morning, most of them on their ordinary everyday journey to work.

The cloudless rain of death

Up in the highlands of equatorial Africa, near the border of Cameroon with Nigeria, there are volcanic crater lakes, some, like Lake Nios, extremely deep.

The night of August 21, 1986, when everyone in the surrounding villages was asleep, something – a strong wind, a little landslide, a tiny earthquake – disturbed Nios. A wave of 200,000 tonnes of water exploded as high as seventy-five metres up the mountainside. Worse, it sent a cataclysmic cloud of water vapour and gas – 2,500,000 cubic metres – down over the silent villages.

Sule Umare, a young cattle herder, remembers. "We thought that rain was coming. I went out and saw the moon shining. I wondered about how rain could come without clouds: I started exclaiming, 'Allah Akbar!' and then I fell." Inside their huts his family and neighbours died where they lay. The cloud killed 1,746 people and all their animals, leaving 10,000 burnt, injured and penniless.

Carbon dioxide seeps through the earth's crust in this part of the world, and is dissolved in the lakes. In deep ones, extra amounts of gas are forced into solution at the lake bottom by huge pressure, and at near-saturation become unstable. Anything can trigger a catastrophic release of gas, which rises to the surface and bursts out – like a monstrous, lethal, fizzy drink.

Refugees from the region around Lake Nios are rescued from the stricken area.

The story of

Omayra Sanches was twelve, a laughing tomboy, top of her class and captain of the baseball team. She never knew she became a symbol courage and hope.

She lived in Armero, Columbia, east of the Nevado del Ruiz, a three-cratered volcano 5,400 metres high in the central range of the Andes in South America. Armero, near Bogota, was a sleepy, prosperous town growing rice and coffee on the fertile soil of the Nevado's 1845 eruption.

The November 1985 blast was small, the kind that happens about fifteen times a year around the world. But it melted eight per cent of the great ice cap, releasing a mudflow metres thick that overwhelmed a huge area and obliterated the whitewashed houses of Armero in a flat sea of grey. At least 25,000 people died, including 8,000 children.

Omayra came to represent them all. She endured three days neck-deep in stinking mud with her feet on her aunt's dead body, while rescuers,

watched by the world's cameras, struggled to free her. She was cheerful and brave and nearly made it: but

ne little girl

as she slipped into a coma she said, "God is calling me now," and she was dead when they at last succeeded. Everywhere people cried for her, and her picture was pinned to every classroom wall in Columbia.

Rescuers attempt to pull Omayra Sanches from the mud

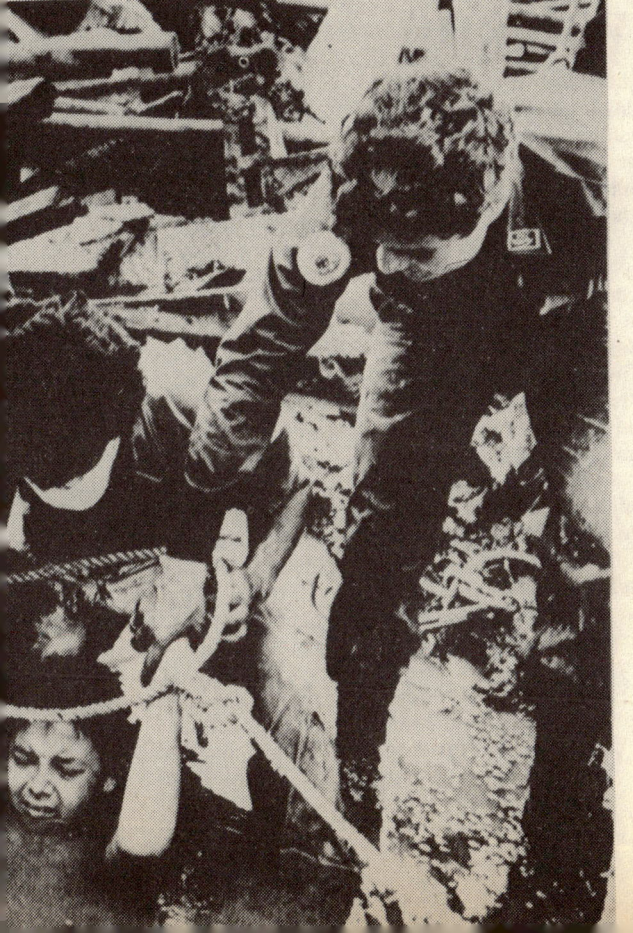

The deadly power of a baby volcano

As everyone in Europe complained about the record-breaking cold, wet weeks of June and July, 1980, some people wondered if it could all be due to the dust veil sent up into the atmosphere by the eruption of Mount St Helens, Washington, in the north-west corner of the United States.

The explosion, at 8.30 a.m. one Sunday in May, probably came too late to affect that summer's weather seriously, and was not as devastating as it might have been, but the force that sent a cloud of hot ash nineteen kilometres into the sky was reckoned to be about the same as that from Mount Vesuvius which buried Pompeii.

For those whose homes were in the area, for the logging camps and their workers and for those who were hiking in the very lovely countryside (even forty-eight kilometres from the peak, which, in spite of warnings, they may have thought was far enough away), the eruption was a murderous disaster. Even with evacuation of the whole area, it killed at least thirty-two people.

The blast tore off the peak of the mountain, leaving it with a flat top 409 metres lower, and sending out about six cubic kilometres of debris. It blew down 241 square kilometres of timber worth about $200,000,000, destroyed crops as far east as Montana, and buried 9,494 kilometres of roads under ash. Outside the area of total devastation, the windborne ash choked towns to a standstill hundreds of kilometres east of the mountain, and in places as far away as Spokane, Washington, 402 kilometres away, the sky was as black as the darkest night. About ninety-six kilometres nearer the volcano, the little town of Ritzville had thirteen centimetres of ash descending on everything, and forming great drifts in the streets, as a current of the warm dust-filled air hit a cold air current from the east. Everywhere traffic was halted by the ashy dust, and once wet the ash turned into a horrible sort

of cement that was almost impossible to shift.

Geologically, Mount St Helens is just a baby volcano, born only 37,000 years ago. It last erupted in 1857, long before people lived, worked or played on it, and we know it has more eruptions still in store for us.

Fire dance

It seems particularly cruel that it is often young people out for an evening's fun who are trapped by fires.

St Laurent du Pont, near Grenoble in France, was too small in 1970 to offer much entertainment, and the Cinq-Sept, where local teenagers went dancing one night, was really just a barn. It had no dance licence, no fire inspection, no water, no telephone, no windows, and the only free exit was a turnstile. It was a death-trap: when a match fell on a cushion, fire swept through it in minutes. It was 1.45 am and half the kids had gone home, but of the 150 left only six got out – a devastating tragedy for a little town.

It was Friday the 13th when youngsters set out for the Stardust Ballroom, Dublin, to dance through the night into St Valentine's Day, 1981. Half-past one, and the end of the disco-dancing competition: someone slashed a seat and set fire to it, and the hall was suddenly an inferno. Forty-eight of the young dancers were killed, and Ireland declared a national day of mourning. One distraught mother was told too late that her three missing children were in fact safe – she collapsed with the strain of waiting and died.

The Statuto cinema, in a working-class area of Turin, is popular with young people because of its cheap prices. In February 1983, the week of Italy's national carnival, many of those watching a French comedy, *The Goat*, were in cheerful fancy dress and make-up. The fire started in the stalls, but it was in the balcony, where the deadly fumes from the plastic seat-covers rose, that most of the sixty-four victims were trapped – some huddled in the toilets.

In each of these fires the youngsters died from the toxic fumes of modern furnishings, from the lack of fire-fighting equipment, and from a common fear of gate-crashers, so that escape routes were heavily locked and barred.

As one fire officer said, when you go to a disco, have a great time, but check all the exits first!

The burning bush

Like California and the French Riviera, south-east Australia never has a summer without a bush fire, but the two-day holocaust in February 1983 was the most terrifying for half a century. With no rain for several years, temperatures of 42°C, winds of 100 kph, and the exploding oil of eucalyptus trees providing fuel, the hill fires around Adelaide and Melbourne created scenes from a desolate war zone.

Seventy people died as their townships were wiped out, 8,000 were homeless, 70,000 hectares of farm and forest land and 200,000 sheep and cattle were destroyed – total damage was about £500,000,000. The oddest victims were 30,000 goldfish (on a goldfish farm!) when a tree fell on their open tanks. The most miraculous survivors were eighty-three who had squeezed into a concrete storm drain.

Power lines touching in high winds sparked some of the fires, others – as happens each year in France – began in uncleared scrub or were

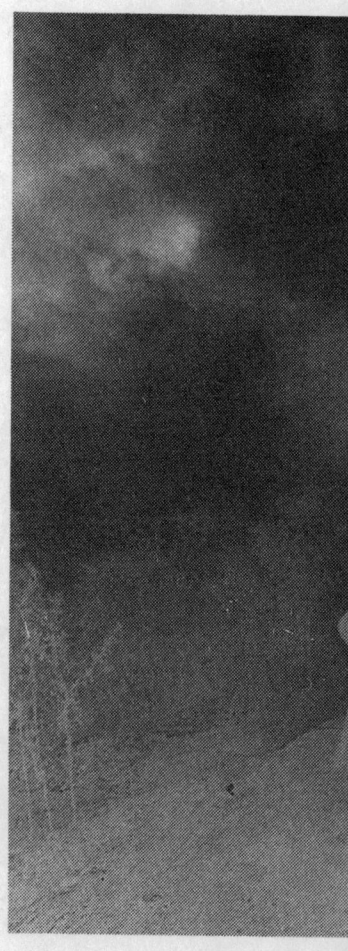

started deliberately by arsonists. "These people are murderers. Would you prefer to be stabbed in the back or boiled alive in a vat of eucalyptus oil?" raged one victim.

As a volunteer fireman said, "It was man versus nature, and although it may sound dramatic, no amount of resources or of bravery would have helped. Nature overwhelmed us."

No sporting chance

Saturday, May 11, 1985, was going to be Bradford's day of celebration, when their football team would be promoted to the English Second Division. Instead, it was a day of stunned grief.

A little before half-time in the match against Lincoln City, someone dropped a light or cigarette through a gap in the wooden floor of the main stand, where it smouldered among years of accumulated rubbish (they later found stuff marked in *pre-decimal* money). But flames quickly appeared among the seats and within minutes fire had swooped across the roof and engulfed the whole stand.

At first people just stood and watched – when they realized the danger it was too late. Fire extinguishers had been removed because vandals used to throw them; and the gates at the back, where many fled, were locked to prevent anyone getting in free, so dozens were trapped there. Most survivors ran on to the pitch, where the television cameras filming the game caught dramatic pictures of people burning like torches

as the blazing roof tarpaulin fell and clung to their clothes.

It had been, of course, a family occasion, and among the fifty-six dead were several fathers and their two children; one eleven-year-old died with his father, grandfather and uncle. The youngest of the many heroes of the fire was ten-year-old Joanne Baron, who received a bravery award for rescuing an elderly man in spite of being burnt herself.

Racing against a ferocious sea

The 974-kilometre Fastnet Race has had more influence on ocean sailing than any other race anywhere. It takes yachts from Cowes, on the Isle of Wight, off the south coast of England, over to the Fastnet Rock at the southern tip of Ireland, and back again to Plymouth, Devon.

The 1979 race was the twenty-eighth since it was started in 1925, and there were 303 starters, crewed by 2,500 sailors from twenty-one countries, the boats ranging in size but all eager to test themselves on what has become the sailor's Mount Everest.

They set off on August 11,

and by the morning of the 14th it was realised on shore that things had gone nastily wrong. The big yachts were in trouble, with twenty-one limping home retired. What must be happening to the smaller boats, those between six and ten metres?

Later, survivors and the hard-pressed (and astonishingly brave) rescue services told what had been happening. Waves twelve to fifteen metres from crest to trough – taller than the yachts' masts – were smashing down on the

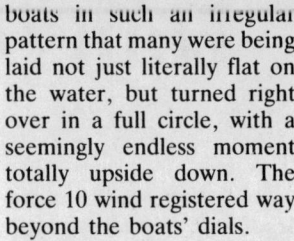

boats in such an irregular pattern that many were being laid not just literally flat on the water, but turned right over in a full circle, with a seemingly endless moment totally upside down. The force 10 wind registered way beyond the boats' dials.

Neither crews nor boats could stand such battering. People were flung about and badly injured, and several were swept away in spite of safety harnesses. Some crews took the understandable, but fatal, decision to abandon what seemed like a doomed boat and use the liferaft: the boats survived, the rafts sometimes did not, or men were swept off them. Hypothermia (when the body temperature sinks too low from the cold and wet) and exhaustion killed some. Others were swept away in the very moment of rescue, trying to climb a ship's ladder.

Only eighty-four boats finished the race – one Frenchman was given an honorary second place for giving up his chances in order to rescue, against all dangers, the crew of another boat. Fifteen men died, and others were unbelievably lucky to survive. Later, sailors who had rounded the Horn or faced a hurricane in a yacht, said they had never known a worse sea.

Hang down your

Two weeks after the fire in the Bradford City stadium, football suffered another, literally savage, blow. Liverpool were playing the Italian team Juventus in the European Cup Final at the Heysel stadium in Brussels. English fans crossed to Belgium in their rowdy thousands: noisy and ferociously drunk, maybe, but surely none was thinking of murder.

Unusually (and unwisely), some Juventus fans were placed in the Liverpool end of the ground, separated from Liverpool by a "neutral" area whose Belgian tickets had found their way on to the black market – allowing their Liverpool buyers to overcrowd their own section while leaving gaps in the neutral area. This gave the belligerent English fans room to pick up speed and charge the isolated Italians, breaking feeble barriers and gathering weapons on the way.

Some Juventus fans fled in terror to the pitch, but others, pushed from the top, were crushed against the terrace barriers. The end wall, crumbling with age, collapsed, and

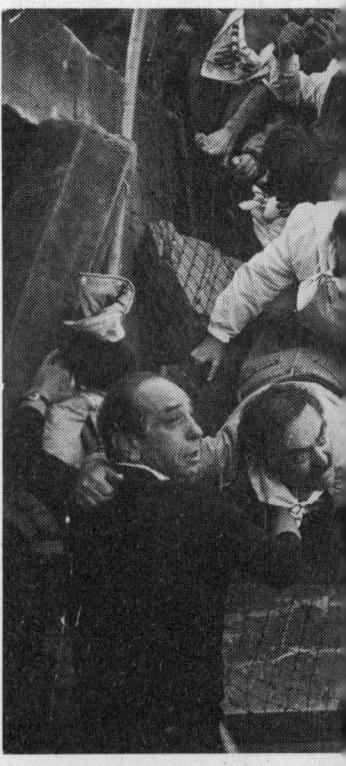

scores of bodies tumbled down amid the concrete. Riot police, arriving too late to prevent the trouble, laid into everyone. For half an hour there was chaos; the Red Cross did their best with first aid, but it was forty minutes before the first stretcher came.

head and cry

Thirty-three Italians, including one ten-year-old, died, and four Belgians, one Frenchman and a casual British visitor at his first football match.

The brutality of those fans branded England in the eyes of the whole world. All English clubs were banned from European cup games for at least three years, Liverpool for even longer. Twenty-two Liverpool supporters, largely identified from television pictures, stood trial in Belgium – accused, some said, of killing football.

The cold, cold face of the Eiger

The Eiger (3,970 metres) in the Swiss Alps, has a terrifying North Face, with about 1,830 metres of vertical precipice, no sun, and is constantly swept by avalanches and falling stones. The first men to try to climb it were two Germans in 1935, who froze to death in their bivouac at 3,350 metres after five days of climbing and clinging to icy ledges.

A year later two young Austrians, who had already tried once, joined with two twenty-three-year-old Germans – all were superb climbers. They discovered what was to be the key to climbing the Eiger, swinging across a holdless stretch of rock by pick and rope, but then drew in the rope afterwards, so making their retreat impossible. No climber would make that mistake again, and the route was named after their leader as a memorial to him.

One of them was injured, and the retreat began, but after three nights up there the weather worsened. Without their earlier rope route, they had to try to lower themselves directly down to a narrow ledge from where they could reach a window into the railway that runs through the Eiger. Their leader fell – straight down through the air below. The second man was snatched up by his connecting rope and hung there until he died, frozen, an hour later. The third, the injured one, hurtled down in a loop of rope and strangled, then, loosened somehow, his body fell 915 metres to the foot of the mountain. The fourth was left dangling in mid-air.

The climbers had been warned that no one would rescue them, but in spite of this two guides set out to try. The first effort was useless, and the climber had to survive another night. In the morning they tried again,

and, agonizing hours later, had inched themselves as close as they could to an impassable overhang. Above they could see the stranded climber's boots – they could almost touch them with an ice axe – but, with his left arm sticking out rigidly from his body, his right hand useless, and his lips so frozen they couldn't understand his replies, it was too much to ask in the end. He suddenly said, quite clearly, "I'm finished," and sagged forward: they could now touch his stiffened legs hanging down, but it was too late to save his life.

The North Face was conquered in 1938. Today the lessons of the past combined with modern techniques seem to have mastered it totally – at the cost of forty-three lives. It knows, this "meanest mountain on earth", there will be more.

Spectator massacre

It promised to be a record-smashing race, with the world's toughest drivers and car manufacturers battling for the honours. The record it eventually held was a more tragic one.

The Le Mans is one of the world's classic twenty-four-hour races, and is held every year in France. There is still argument about whose, if any one person's, fault it was on that evening in June, 1955, but put very simply what happened was this:

British driver Mike Hawthorn lapped another British driver, Lance Macklin, and then pulled in for a pit stop. Behind Macklin was a Frenchman, Pierre Levegh, who was about to be lapped himself by world champion Juan Fangio. Macklin, unable to slow behind Hawthorn in time, pulled over to the left, and Levegh's car hit his rear and took off about five metres into the air before hitting the bank and a crown of spectators. Fangio just squeezed between it and Macklin's car.

Levegh's crashed car exploded. Its rear axle flew among the crown and decapitated some people while others were hit by the engine and covered in burning petrol.

Not only was the driver Levegh killed, but eighty-two spectators died too, and many more were injured. The disaster was so ghastly that all motor racing was banned throughout Europe for four months, and the safety of those who watch was for the first time given the attention it deserved.

Swinging disasters

A fourteen-year-old girl was the only survivor when a cable car packed with forty-three skiers crashed near the resort of Cavalese, north Italy, in March 1976. The cabin fell ninety metres into a dry riverbed when the cable was "cut like a piece of salami" in this worst of all ski-lift accidents, for which four men were later jailed.

That same month, at Vail, in Colorado, USA, a broken cable sent two cars crashing down, leaving one suspended on a strip of steel three millimetres thick. Four people were killed, and ski patrols had to rescue 176 others swinging seventy metres in the air.

Actually, ski-lift crashes are quite rare. So Italy felt hounded by fate when, on the very day of the dreadful cinema fire in Turin (page 94), high winds caused three cars to plunge sixty metres into a mountainside near fashionable Champoluc, above the Valle d'Aosta. Eight adults and two children died, and passengers stranded at 1,876 metres were winched to safety by helicopters.

On March 1, 1987, the concrete block holding the main chair lift pylon gave way at Luz-Ardiden, a small Pyrenées resort on the scenic route between Lourdes and the Spanish border. The whole cable length fell, throwing fifty cars to the ground; some skiers were flung out into the snow, others on to rocks where they bounced and fell again – five were killed and 117 injured. This brand new lift had sophisticated electronic safety checks – all made useless by a poor mixture of concrete.

A cruel Christmas gift from Tracey

Even by the mighty standards of Australia, Darwin, perched at the top of the Northern Territory, is a faraway, independent, kind of a place.

Generally speaking, this part of the world gets three tropical cyclones a year. Some merely dissolve into torrential rainstorms, but some cause a lot of damage. And every so often, one brings catastrophe.

Cyclone Tracey was first noticed on December 21, 1974. (Down under, Christmas comes in the middle of summer.) No one was especially bothered, because only three weeks earlier, Cyclone Selma – all over the world hurricanes are given names in alphabetical order, although they don't any longer have to be girls' names – had threatened Darwin but then turned away out to sea. But by Christmas Eve, cyclone warnings were being regularly broadcast, sirens were wailing every quarter of an hour and the wind had risen into gusts of 100 kph.

Still, people were thinking more about Christmas next day than the weather, and trusting in the government building regulations to ensure that their homes were safe. In fact, most people in Darwin at that time – about 41,000 – lived in wooden houses on stilts.

At 2.30 a.m. the wind suddenly stopped, bringing a strong frightening quiet which lasted for half an hour. Then . . . Tracey struck. The airport wind gauge broke, but gusts were up to 320 kph. Planes were piled up in a tangled heap, trains and trucks were hurled around, and the entire town was flattened. People sheltered as best they could – in old deep freezers, under beds, in the lavatory. . . .

Miraculously only forty-nine died, with 300 injured, but the subsequent chaos, the threat of disease, the shock and the lack of food were the real problems. Over 17,000 victims were airlifted out, and many, though they had lost

everything, were happy at the thought of never seeing Darwin again. The rest stubbornly set about rebuilding their town again – but more securely this time.

Way over to the east of Darwin, in the South Pacific, cyclone Namu tore through the Solomon Islands in May 1986, with two days of winds up to 185 kmh. Hundreds died and 100,000 were left homeless, while epidemics and the destruction of the country's "rice bowl" in the Guadalcanal Plains suggested a far bleaker future for the islanders than Darwin's.

Alpine terror

The people who live on and patrol the mountain slopes of the Alps have learned a lot about controlling snow avalanches. Where and when to set them off deliberately, so that they fall before they grow too huge and uncontrollable, when to evacuate houses, how to find buried victims. . . all this is dangerous and skilled work.

The weather, however, sometimes defeats any efforts ordinary human beings can make. January 1951 was like that: in the eastern section of the high Alps, but north of

the St Gotthard pass – an area sprinkled with names that suggest only carefree skiing holidays to the rest of the world – almost three metres of snow fell in the ten days up to January 22, with an unbelievable two metres in the last seven days. Some places had ten to fifteen centimetres falling in only one hour, and it was so thick as to be almost suffocating.

Everywhere in the villages people waited, watched and

worried. They knew that up above them the massive avalanches were poised, yet conditions were too appalling for the usual patrols to forestall any onslaught, and many brave men died in one avalanche as they were trying to rescue the victim of a previous one.

Andermatt had five avalanches roar down into the village itself, and four on its outskirts, all within a few days. There were 1,100 in the entire area, and in the canton of Graubunden alone there were 649, with fifty-four people killed.

Then two weeks later, it started to snow again, but this time centring on the Ticino canton, south of the St Gotthard. In Bedretto, in the 24 hours of February 12, an Alpine record of one-and-a-quarter metres of snow fell. The little town of Airolo was particularly badly hit, with ten people killed and twenty-nine buildings destroyed.

In that one short stretch of winter in the Alps, 279 people were killed by avalanches, 285 were injured, 1,400 cattle died and more than half the native wild life was wiped out. Many surviving villagers were left with a lifelong fear of hearing again the terrible noise of an approaching avalanche.

Death twisters

Tornadoes are the most powerful natural killers in the world. Hurricanes do more damage, because they rage over a much wider area, but with its whirling winds of 240–320 kph (some have reached an unbelievable 800 kph) and a central vacuum that *explodes* houses as well as hurling them down, there's nothing as vicious as a tornado.

The intense pressure inside a tornado centre turns harmless objects, like wooden splinters and straws, into weapons. Gravel and sand are embedded in people's bodies, and a horse was once killed by a corn cob piercing its skull.

At dusk on May 31, 1985, twenty-seven tornadoes cut a swathe sixty metres wide and

480 kilometres long, through the US states of Pennsylvania, Ohio, west New York and – unusually – up into Ontario in Canada, virtually destroying several small towns. Although forecasting normally gives warnings (back in 1925 the "Tri-State Tornado" killed 600), these storms moved too fast to prevent the ninety-three deaths and 550 injured – the worst toll since 315 were killed in the Mid-West in one night of 1974.

The narrow path of a tornado is capricious in choosing victims. In Wheatland, Pennsylvania, thirty-two-year-old David Kostka was umpiring a junior baseball game when the tornado struck. He flung his little niece and playmate into a ditch and himself on top of them: he saved their lives but *he* was snatched away like a matchstick. Not far away, eight women at a Tupperware party rushed for the storm cellar – one didn't make it, and was found three kilometres away in a creek.

But there were also miracles. In Albion a mother couldn't reach her two-year-old before the sides of her house were blown away, but she and the baby were safe while twelve of her unlucky neighbours died.

Attention! Mice advancing. . .

When the farmers first came across the waves of mice on their land, it was their crops they were worrying about. Theirs was the wheat-growing belt of the Mallee, in the state of Victoria in the south-east corner of Australia, and never before had mice been known to eat crops that were actually growing.

The first plague of common house mice was in 1969, and not only were they attacking the stored foods but puzzling everyone by doing enormous damage to the sheep's stubble grazing, the growing rice and maize as well as fruit and vegetables. They were like a moving carpet in places, and a farmer could trap 300 or 400 in a night! All anyone could do was wait for winter and hope the frosts would kill them off, or that they would eat each other.

Ten years later they were back. October brought the first signs of invasion, and a Ministry of Agriculture warning of the building-up of mouse movement. But this time the mice weren't content with eating the harvest, they moved indoors. People found that "there were dead mice in the bath and sinks and in the water tanks. Children in their sleep were having their hair pulled out to line the mice's nests."

One farming family went on holiday in February 1980 (summer in Australia) and came back to find their house devastated:

Cushions, blankets, bedspreads, clothes in drawers and on hangers, were all eaten. Dead mice were in drawers, mattresses, under pillows, under furniture. Mice manure was piled in the corners, over the stove, one-and-a-quarter centimetres thick around the kitchen benches and on all the windowsills. . .

No one knows where they came from – nor when they'll come again.

The battle of the crocodiles

The Saltwater Crocodile, about six metres long, is one of the most vicious animals in the world. It lives off-shore, from south-east Asia to Australia, and is far more dangerous than the shark. Crocodiles hunt large prey, and since they can't chew, they tear a body apart by spinning round while they hold one limb.

Towards the end of World War II, the British had trapped over 1,000 Japanese infantrymen on the edge of a mangrove swamp on Ramree Island, which you can see on a map, off the west coast of Burma. From the air the twenty-nine kilometres between this large island and the mainland looks like solid land, but in fact it is a waist-deep swamp infested with giant saltwater crocodiles. By February 19, 1945, the Japanese had been cornered in this swamp as they tried to escape from the British troops on the island.

The noise of battle brought all the crocodiles from far and wide into the water, where they lay becoming more and more excited by the scent of blood. That night, when the firing had stopped, the tide crept out and the crocodiles crept in – in to where the Japanese were caught knee-deep in the muck and swamp-water.

All night the British could hear the tremendous thrashing as the monsters spun round with their victims, dead and alive, and the screaming of the soldiers. Of the original 1,000 men, only twenty survived: some, of course, had been shot and some drowned, but it was the crocodiles who had really won that battle.

Killer buzz

In 1956 well-meaning scientists brought some African queen bees to Rio Claro in São Paulo in Brazil, to try to develop a more productive bee. Only a year later twenty-six swarms had escaped, headed by African queens.

They crossbreed very easily with European bees, and the hybrid swarms spread incredibly quickly. This is partly because they are very, very fierce, and are quite prepared to launch unprovoked mass attacks on any animals and people in their path, and to rob other bees' nests. Their stings are dangerous – indeed, often fatal – both to animals and humans.

They swarm more frequently than ordinary bees, and move on all the time, and they have already reached the southern parts of the United States – and since a bee isn't very likely to fly in a literal "bee-line", that must mean at *least* 11,000 kilometres. Only the fact that they don't survive wintry weather might defeat them.

A man-eater's last stand

There's probably no more terrifying animal, either in one's mind or in real life, than a man-eating tiger. Yet by nature these huge, powerful and swift beasts are dignified and unaggressive with humans and certainly have no taste for human meat.

But when an animal's speed and the condition of its teeth and claws are damaged by wounds – or by old age, though this is less common than one would think – it is sometimes driven by hunger to attack humans, who are easier to catch. Apart from gunshot wounds, porcupine quills can often not only blind a tiger but embed themselves agonisingly in its legs and pads. About fifty quills can enter the skin, some up to twenty centimetres long, and if they hit a bone they can double back in a U-turn and their ends break off, so that the wretched animal can't get them out with its teeth. The wounds, of course, fester and go bad.

In the twenties and thirties – when tigers were much more common than they are today (for in some parts now these proud and beautiful animals are almost extinct) – one particular man, Jim Corbett, was famous for his knowledge of the jungle and hills of India, and for his uncanny skills in hunting. When a tiger turned man-eater, terrorising villagers who had to tend their cattle and cut grass every day knowing that somewhere, unseen, the tiger was trailing them as prey, the village chiefs and district authorities would send for Corbett to help them.

Corbett admired and respected tigers, but he had seen the appalling bloody remains of people – from young girls to old men – who had been carried off by desperate animals, and he was relentlessly patient in his hunting, even if it took weeks and weeks. It was dangerous work, for a man-eater loses all its usual fear of humans, and is only too ready to stand its ground.

One of his most awesome

kills was a tigress who had been driven out of Nepal after two years of man-eating, and who then for another two years brought terror to the district around Naini Tal. (You can find Naini Tal, and near it Amora – the head-quarters that had sent out Ghurka soldiers to try to kill the tigress – marked on an atlas, high in the hills of Uttar Pradesh, in India, close to the western border of Nepal.) Jim Corbett tracked the tigress as she dragged a sixteen-year-old girl over a wilderness of rocks. The girl was dead – luckily, for some-times man-eaters are no longer capable of killing their victims at once, and people are carried away screaming for help, or else they escape and die only later, slowly, from their terrible wounds.

This girl was the tigress's 436th human kill and, after Jim Corbett had cornered her, the last.

The tragic end of the kouprey

Usually, especially in modern times, it is man who inflicts disaster on animals, not the other way round. And among the innocent victims of war-torn Cambodia, now Kampuchea, is the kouprey.

The kouprey, or Cambodian forest ox, is – maybe we should now say *was* – unique. One of the most ancient of the bovids (the cattle family), it is a "living fossil" with certain extremely primitive features – its molars, for instance, are most like those of *Proleptarbus*, an extinct fossil ox. It is probably the closest living link to the missing ancestors of the Indian hump cattle. At any rate, as a "gene-bank" developed over 100,000 years, it is of uncountable value to the world of science.

Up to June 1970 it was thought that some kouprey – perhaps between about thirty and seventy – had survived in the north–eastern forests of Cambodia, near the border with Vietnam. But there is little chance that they could have lived through the terrible events that have since happened there, in spite of the years of care and conservation the Cambodians had given them until then.

They lived in an area where the Vietcong lived off the land, and the American forces destroyed the land. Bombs, defoliation (that means killing all vegetation) and poison gas released by retreating American troops: how could a few kouprey hope to survive?

Photographs of the same area of jungle show the devastating effects of aerial spraying with defoliant.

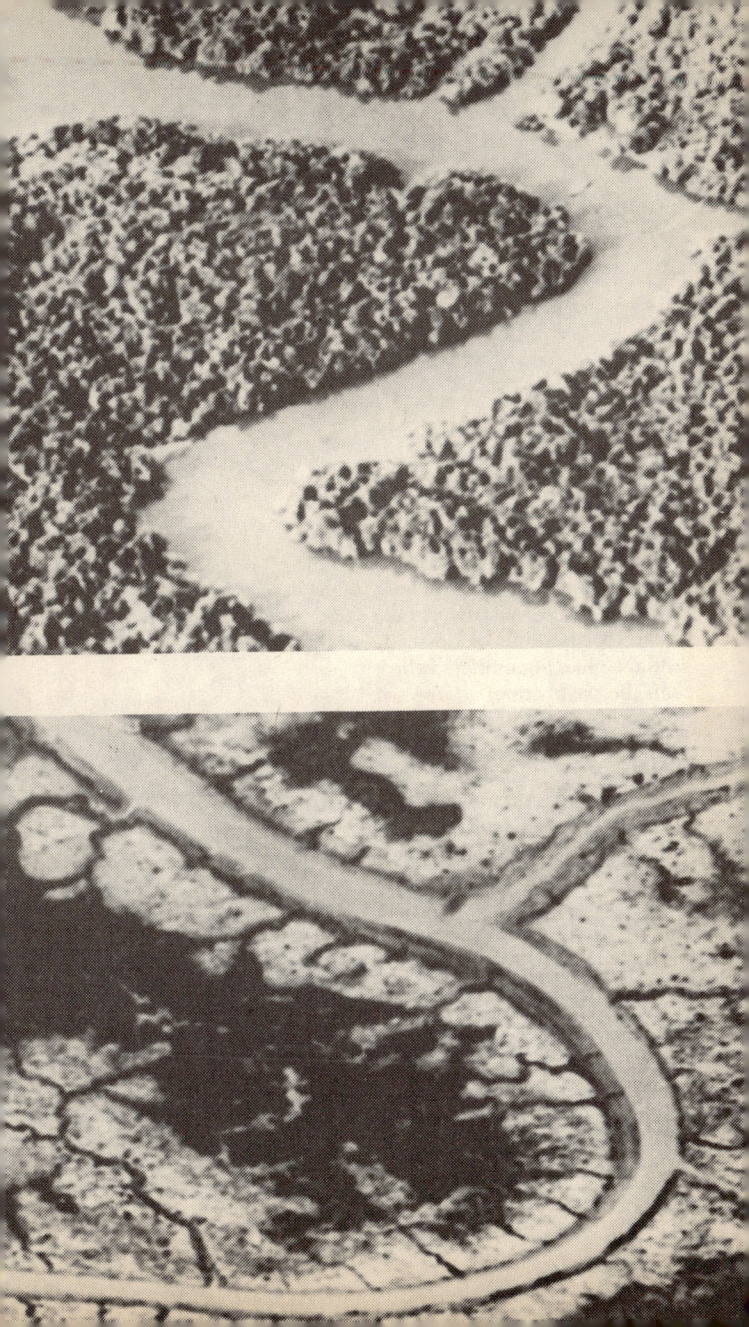

The war both sides lost

Most of us don't take a bout of flu too seriously, but that is only because we are lucky enough to live in an age of antibiotics. These can usually take care of the kind of developments, like pneumonia, which in the past turned an unpleasant illness into a killing one.

At the end of the First World War, 1918–19, the mingling together in northern France of troops from all over Europe, America and Africa was the perfect breeding ground for an epidemic which soon swept round the world. It was caused by some new, particularly tough, strains of flu virus, and, after the years of war and poor food the generally weakened state of people everywhere made complications like pneumonia even more serious.

Services of all kinds broke

down in almost every country in the world, and people often collapsed in the street and died within days or even hours. The war had killed about 10,000,000 people in four-and-a-half years; flu killed over 20,000,000 in under one year.

An anti-flu spray in use.

Hidden enemy

A strange illness that puzzled doctors killed the Bellvue Stratford Hotel in Philadelphia. The disease was first heard of at the beginning of August 1976, and by November the hotel was dead.

It began when thousands of members of the American Legion attended a state convention in Philadelphia, Pennsylvania, for three days in July 1976. Not long after they were home again, 211 developed an illness rather like flu, and some became extremely ill with a severe form of pneumonia. Thirty-four people actually died, but because they all lived far apart it was a while before anyone connected their deaths with the convention. After that, the disease was called Legionnaires' Disease.

Health inspectors almost tore the hotel apart to find out what caused the disease: they checked the kitchen, the paint, the vinyl, the cleaning polish, the carpets, the air conditioning. . . Nothing. And although there were no more cases, and the disease was quite obviously not infectious, no one would stay at the hotel, in spite of every assurance – including the President himself deliberately staying there to prove its safety. Finally, the hotel was forced to close.

Since then scientists have been stalking the bug that causes *Legionella pneumophila*, which is probably not new at all but was simply confused before with pneumonia. It is actually everywhere – all soils, most surface water – but like all microbes it has a delicate, complicated lifestyle, and at a crucial point, between very specifically 30°C and 55°C and in very particular situations, it can multiply ferociously and invade.

Fine water droplets (which can be breathed in) from shower heads, drainpipes and the cooling towers of air conditioning systems can offer the right conditions, so we now know that what's important is to keep all water systems clean by chlorination.

In 1985 an English hospital, Stafford General District, which was opened only two years before, had the worst recorded outbreak, with forty-six deaths. Over Easter the air conditioning was switched off, and when it was later restarted, bacteria were blown over patients and visitors. Some were perfectly fit and only in the building for fifteen minutes: the tiniest exposure to one droplet is all this fastidious bug needs.

New York City Sanitation Department officials cleaning the streets with extra care following a new outbreak of the mysterious Legionnaires' disease.

Acknowledgements

The photographs in this book are reproduced with the permission of: Ardea: 121; Associated Press: 91; Australian Office of Information: 111; Barnaby's Picture Library: 84; Camera Press: 114; the Keystone Collection: front and back covers, 8, 13, 27, 41, 49, 60, 71; Novosti Press: 73, 75; Popperfoto: 19, 21, 35, 39, 45, 50, 67, 69, 78, 80, 93, 112, 123, 127; Press Association: 57, 87, 100; Radio Times Hulton Picture Library: 25, 47, 52, 63, 64, 83, 106, 125; Rex Features: 14, 16, 22, 29, 31, 33, 37, 55, 60, 89, 95, 97, 99, 103, 108; Swiss National Tourist Office: 105; John Topham: 117, 118.